ISBN 0-8373-0757-0

C-757   CAREER EXAMINATION SERIES

This is your PASSBOOK® for...

State Trooper

Test Preparation Study Guide

Questions & Answers

NLC

NATIONAL LEARNING CORPORATION

Copyright © 2013 by

National Learning Corporation

212 Michael Drive, Syosset, New York 11791

(516) 921-8888
(800) 645-6337
FAX: (516) 921-8743
www.passbooks.com
sales @ passbooks.com
info @ passbooks.com

PRINTED IN THE UNITED STATES OF AMERICA

PASSBOOK®
NOTICE

This book is SOLELY intended for, is sold ONLY to, and its use is RESTRICTED to *individual*, bona fide applicants or candidates who qualify by virtue of having seriously filed applications for appropriate license, certificate, professional and/or promotional advancement, higher school matriculation, scholarship, or other legitimate requirements of educational and/or governmental authorities.

This book is NOT intended for use, class instruction, tutoring, training, duplication, copying, reprinting, excerption, or adaptation, etc., by:

(1) Other publishers

(2) Proprietors and/or Instructors of "Coaching" and/or Preparatory Courses

(3) Personnel and/or Training Divisions of commercial, industrial, and governmental organizations

(4) Schools, colleges, or universities and/or their departments and staffs, including teachers and other personnel

(5) Testing Agencies or Bureaus

(6) Study groups which seek by the purchase of a single volume to copy and/or duplicate and/or adapt this material for use by the group as a whole without having purchased individual volumes for each of the members of the group

(7) Et al.

Such persons would be in violation of appropriate Federal and State statutes.

PROVISION OF LICENSING AGREEMENTS. — Recognized educational commercial, industrial, and governmental institutions and organizations, and others legitimately engaged in educational pursuits, including training, testing, and measurement activities, may address a request for a licensing agreement to the copyright owners, who will determine whether, and under what conditions, including fees and charges, the materials in this book may be used by them. In other words, a licensing facility exists for the legitimate use of the material in this book on other than an individual basis. However, it is asseverated and affirmed here that the material in this book *CANNOT* be used without the receipt of the express permission of such a licensing agreement from the Publishers.

NATIONAL LEARNING CORPORATION
212 Michael Drive
Syosset, New York 11791

Inquiries re licensing agreements should be addressed to:
The President
National Learning Corporation
212 Michael Drive
Syosset, New York 11791

PASSBOOK® SERIES

THE *PASSBOOK® SERIES* has been created to prepare applicants and candidates for the ultimate academic battlefield — the examination room.

At some time in our lives, each and every one of us may be required to take an examination — for validation, matriculation, admission, qualification, registration, certification, or licensure.

Based on the assumption that every applicant or candidate has met the basic formal educational standards, has taken the required number of courses, and read the necessary texts, the *PASSBOOK® SERIES* furnishes the one special preparation which may assure passing with confidence, instead of failing with insecurity. Examination questions — together with answers — are furnished as the basic vehicle for study so that the mysteries of the examination and its compounding difficulties may be eliminated or diminished by a sure method.

This book is meant to help you pass your examination provided that you qualify and are serious in your objective.

The entire field is reviewed through the huge store of content information which is succinctly presented through a provocative and challenging approach — the question-and-answer method.

A climate of success is established by furnishing the correct answers at the end of each test.

You soon learn to recognize types of questions, forms of questions, and patterns of questioning. You may even begin to anticipate expected outcomes.

You perceive that many questions are repeated or adapted so that you can gain acute insights, which may enable you to score many sure points.

You learn how to confront new questions, or types of questions, and to attack them confidently and work out the correct answers.

You note objectives and emphases, and recognize pitfalls and dangers, so that you may make positive educational adjustments.

Moreover, you are kept fully informed in relation to new concepts, methods, practices, and directions in the field.

You discover that you are actually taking the examination all the time: you are preparing for the examination by "taking" an examination, not by reading extraneous and/or supererogatory textbooks.

In short, this PASSBOOK®, used directedly, should be an important factor in helping you to pass your test.

STATE TROOPER

DUTIES

The work of the State Police ranges from traditional patrol duties to those of specially trained investigators conducting sophisticated operations against drug traffickers and other criminals. The Uniformed Force has two primary responsibilities: to protect life and property; and to promote highway safety. In many areas of the state, Uniformed Troopers are the primary law enforcement officers and respond to all types of calls including burglaries, missing children, assaults, robberies, and homicides. Troopers not only enforce the Vehicle and Traffic Laws, but in many of the town courts in the state will act on behalf of the District Attorney's Office to prosecute the case. Usually on misdemeanor level crimes, the trooper conducts the entire investigation and works with the District Attorney's Office during the prosecution phase. For felony cases, troopers conduct the preliminary investigation and have an opportunity, while working closely with investigators assigned to the Bureau of Criminal Investigation, to develop leads that may help solve the case.

CRITICAL AND FREQUENT TASKS OF A TROOPER

- Operates a motor vehicle in all types of weather.
- Carries a firearm as a job requirement.
- Determines action to be taken in emergency situations.
- Patrols within a wide geographic area, such as highways, waterways, and woodlands.
- Provides direction and information to the public.
- Assists motorists, enforces traffic laws and investigates accidents.
- Assesses personal injury situations, renders first aid, and provides or arranges transportation to medical facilities.
- Responds to all types of offenses including crimes in progress, civil matters, domestic disputes, property crimes, and serious crimes.
- Investigates felony and misdemeanor crimes.
- Notes and investigates suspicious activity.
- Interviews witnesses, victims, and others to obtain information.
- Conducts searches of individuals, automobiles, occupancies, etc., when necessary.
- Obtains and analyzes information, collects physical evidence, and participates in the judicial process of criminal and noncriminal investigations.
- Obtains or serves summonses, warrants, or other legal documents.
- Apprehends, restrains, arrests, transports, and detains suspects.
- Appears in court or before a grand jury as a witness.
- Assumes desk duties.
- Prepares blotter entries and narratives of activities.
- Operates a PIN terminal.
- Provides dignitary protection.
- Cooperates and shares information with other related law enforcement agencies.

SCOPE OF THE EXAMINATION

The written test will consist of multiple-choice questions designed to assess specific cognitive (mental) abilities determined to be important to the effective performance of a State Trooper's job duties. These abilities include:

- Memorization
- Visualization
- Spatial Orientation
- Verbal Comprehension
- Verbal Expression
- Reasoning (inductive and deductive)
- Problem Sensitivity
- Ability to Order Information

HOW TO PREPARE GUIDE FOR

STATE TROOPER

WRITTEN EXAMINATION

I. INTRODUCTION

The job of State Trooper involves general highway patrol and police work in the protection of life and property. Employees in this class are responsible for enforcement of state laws, with special reference to those relating to the use of motor vehicles. Work includes an element of danger, and normally involves making routine patrols of state highways, directing traffic, and investigating accidents and crimes, but may include other specialized police activities. Employees undergo an intense period of training in police methods and in the use of firearms prior to duty assignment. Work is performed in accordance with prescribed regulations and procedures. Instruction and support assistance are available in unusual situations, but employees are required to independently exercise sound judgment in emergencies. Work is checked by supervising officers through inspection and observation.

II. JOB DUTIES

The following is a list of major job duties that new State Troopers must perform upon completion of the Training Academy. These areas of responsibility will give you a general overview of the job.

- Patrols federal, state, and local roadways using patrol vehicle, speed detection radar, emergency equipment, radios, departmental paperwork, and computers following Department of Public Safety (DPS) policies and procedures as needed to enforce traffic laws, assist motorists and accident victims, and identify and mitigate public safety hazards.

- Responds to emergency situations such as single and multiple-vehicular accidents, traffic fatalities, hazardous materials spills, and criminal activity using patrol vehicle, emergency equipment, and communication equipment following DPS policies and procedures as needed to clear roadways, ensure medical assistance for victims, and ensure the safety of the public.

- Investigates collisions/accidents and criminal activities such as driving under the influence or possessing alcoholic beverages and/or illegal drugs to include determining cause of collisions, gathering evidence, and interviewing witnesses using breath analysis equipment (Draeger), field sobriety test, camera, notepad, pen, tape measure, CAD equipment, and computer following DPS policies and procedures as needed to document details of accidents, compose narrative descriptions of events, testify in court, and provide evidence to district attorneys regarding criminal activity.

- Performs general maintenance of equipment and vehicle to include conducting pre-shift and post-shift checks of all equipment and vehicle and monitoring equipment and vehicle during shift using basic tools following DPS policies and procedures and equipment manual specifications as needed to ensure the safe working condition of equipment and vehicle and the neat, professional appearance of equipment, vehicle, and self.

- Performs administrative duties such as logging activities, preparing and maintaining forms and reports, and properly handling legal documents such as tickets using departmental paperwork, computer, and writing utensils following DPS policies and procedures as needed to document all work activities, maintain records of legal actions, and comply with legal and departmental requirements.

- Performs public and community relations such as speaking formally and informally to individual citizens and groups as needed to provide information, assist the public, and present a positive image of the Department of Public Safety.

- Performs professional development activities such as participating in special training, reading law enforcement related publications, attending conferences and seminars, and maintaining physical and technical skill levels using standard-issue equipment, the internet, and departmental guidelines as needed to maintain and improve personal knowledge, skills, and abilities related to the job of State Trooper.

III. WRITTEN EXAM

Applicants who meet the minimum qualifications for the job of State Trooper will be scheduled to take a written, multiple-choice exam. The State Personnel Department will send candidates a postcard in the mail indicating the location and time you are scheduled to take the exam. You will be required to take that postcard along with photo identification to the test site. You will have three hours to complete the exam, and you may leave the test site if you finish the exam before three hours have passed.

The written exam will be administered at various locations throughout the state. Every effort will be made to accommodate your request for preferred exam locations as indicated on your application. Candidates for State Trooper will be assigned to test centers based on the dates their applications are received. So, if you are not scheduled for the exam location preferences that you indicate on your application, those test centers were filled to capacity or closed. In those cases, you were scheduled based on availability at other test centers so that you could take the written exam. If you are not able to participate in the written exam and wish to be rescheduled to take the exam at a later date, you should write "Reschedule" on your original schedule postcard and return it to the State Personnel Department. If you have misplaced your postcard, you can also put your request in writing and send it to the State Personnel Department.

Exam Content

The written exam contains 66 multiple-choice questions divided into five sections. These sections are as follows: Mathematics, English and Proofreading, Logical Ordering of Information, Judgment and Decision Making, and Reading Comprehension. Each question has four options from which to choose the correct answer. There is only one correct answer for each question.

The exam questions were compiled by State Personnel testing experts with assistance from incumbent State Troopers. Incumbent State Troopers reviewed and approved each written exam question and determined that all items: (1) were job-related, (2) measured knowledges or abilities that are important to perform the job of State Trooper, and (3) were good items (i.e., clearly written, unbiased, written on the appropriate level of difficulty). Incumbent State Troopers also were required to provide the correct answers to the exam questions in order for the questions to meet the criteria required for them to be included on the final test.

Each section of the exam, along with instructions and a sample question, is represented on the following pages. The instructions are the actual instructions that will appear on the exam. The sample questions provided are designed to familiarize you with the format of the exam; they will **NOT** appear on the actual exam.

IV. SAMPLE TEST QUESTIONS

Mathematics

This section of the exam is designed to measure your knowledge of basic mathematics. The questions in this section require you to perform addition, subtraction, multiplication, and/or division. For each question, select the correct answer from the options provided. **You are not allowed to use a calculator during the exam.**

1. The roadway you are patrolling has a speed limit of 55 miles per hour.   1.____
   A car passes you at an estimated speed of 68 miles per hour. How many
   miles per hour **above** the speed limit is the car traveling?
   A. 11   B. 12   C. 13   D. 14

English and Proofreading

This section of the exam is designed to measure your knowledge of the English language and your ability to proofread written documents. The questions in this section are related to grammar, spelling, punctuation, capitalization, and appropriate word usage. For each question, select the correct answer from the options provided.

2. Select the most appropriate form of the sentence according to standard   2.____
   English from the options provided below.
   A. I wrote ten tickets while on patrol last night.
   B. During my last night patrol, I wrote ten tickets.
   C. I was on patrol last night when I wrote ten tickets.
   D. On patrol duty last night was when I wrote ten tickets.

Logical Ordering of Information

This section of the exam is designed to measure your ability to identify disorganized information and place the information into logical order. The questions in this section require you to review different types of information and determine the logical order in which the information should be arranged. For each question, select the correct answer from the options provided.

3.   Trooper Jones gathered statements from several witnesses to a car   3.____
      collision. He now has to put the information into logical order to determine
      exactly what occurred. The statements are provided below. (These
      statements are **NOT** listed in the correct order.)
      I.   A blue Suburban turned left out of the parking lot onto Jones Street
           in front of the Honda.
      II. A green Honda was speeding down Jones Street. There was loud
           music coming from the car.
      III. The two cars collided and then the Honda spun off the road into the
           ditch.
      IV. The driver of the Honda did not see the Suburban because he was
           leaning out the window yelling to a girl on the sidewalk.

      The MOST logical order for the sentences to appear in the accident report
      is
      A. I, II, III, IV   B. II, I, IV, III   C. II, III, IV, I   D. I, III, II, IV

Judgment and Decision Making

This section of the exam is designed to measure your ability to make effective judgments and decisions based on available information. In this section, you will be given specific situations that require decisions to be made. You will answer questions about those situations, using the information provided. For each question, select the correct answer from the options provided.

Decision Making Scenario

State Trooper Allen reviewed the post activity log and discovered the following trends about his/her region:

•   Most single car accidents occur on Mondays, Thursdays, and Fridays. Most two-car collisions occur on Tuesdays, Fridays, and Saturdays. Multiple car collisions occur most frequently on Wednesdays, Thursdays, and Sundays.

•   Most single car accidents occur between 6:00 P.M. and Midnight. Most two-car collisions occur between 3:00 P.M. and 8:00 P.M. Most multiple car collisions occur between 7:00 A.M. and 1:00 P.M.

4.   According to the information in the above passage, State Trooper   4.____
      Allen would MOST likely be able to reduce the number of two-car
      collisions by patrolling on
      A. Mondays at 5:00 P.M.   B. Tuesdays at 7:00 P.M.
      C. Wednesdays at 9:00 A.M.   D. Thursdays at 8:30 A.M.

Reading Comprehension

This section of the exam is designed to measure your ability to read materials and understand the information you read. In this section of the exam, you are given several passages to read. You will then answer one or more questions about each reading passage. For each question, select the correct answer from the options provided. Answers to the questions should be based only on information contained in the reading passages and not on prior knowledge of the subject matter.

Training for law enforcement officers has shown that there is a liability risk to the officer and agency if officers are not trained and do not maintain appropriate levels of fitness for performing critical tasks. Untrained offices may put their own lives at risk in carrying out their duties, and they may also be a risk to the general public. Training ensures that officers are competent and able to perform their duties correctly.

5. Which of the following statements BEST summarizes the reading passage?   5.____
    A. Physical fitness is an important part of law enforcement.
    B. Officers are constantly in risky situations when on the job.
    C. Police officers have to worry about liability when performing their duties.
    D. Training is critical in making sure law enforcement officers are good at their jobs and avoid putting themselves and others at risk.

KEY (CORRECT ANSWERS)

1. The correct answer is "C". The car is traveling at 68 miles per hour and the speed limit is 55 miles per hour, so 68 minus 55 equals 13. The car is traveling 13 miles per hour above the speed limit.

2. The correct answer is "A". This sentence reflects the best use of grammar, word usage, and sentence structure of the options provided. It most clearly communicates the intent of the message.

3. The correct answer is "B". If the statements were read in the order of Statement II, then Statement I, then Statement IV, and then Statement III, that order provides the most logical or best description of the incident that occurred on Jones Street.

4. The correct answer is "B". According to the scenario, two-car collisions occur most frequently on Tuesdays, Fridays, and Saturdays between 3:00 P.M. and 8:00 P.M. Of the options provided, only option B, Tuesdays at 7:00 P.M., falls into those days and times.

5. The correct answer is "D". The reading passage focuses on the importance of training, and option "D" best summarizes that information.

HOW TO TAKE A TEST

I. YOU MUST PASS AN EXAMINATION

A. WHAT EVERY CANDIDATE SHOULD KNOW

Examination applicants often ask us for help in preparing for the written test. What can I study in advance? What kinds of questions will be asked? How will the test be given? How will the papers be graded?

As an applicant for a civil service examination, you may be wondering about some of these things. Our purpose here is to suggest effective methods of advance study and to describe civil service examinations.

Your chances for success on this examination can be increased if you know how to prepare. Those "pre-examination jitters" can be reduced if you know what to expect. You can even experience an adventure in good citizenship if you know why civil service exams are given.

B. WHY ARE CIVIL SERVICE EXAMINATIONS GIVEN?

Civil service examinations are important to you in two ways. As a citizen, you want public jobs filled by employees who know how to do their work. As a job seeker, you want a fair chance to compete for that job on an equal footing with other candidates. The best-known means of accomplishing this two-fold goal is the competitive examination.

Exams are widely publicized throughout the nation. They may be administered for jobs in federal, state, city, municipal, town or village governments or agencies.

Any citizen may apply, with some limitations, such as the age or residence of applicants. Your experience and education may be reviewed to see whether you meet the requirements for the particular examination. When these requirements exist, they are reasonable and applied consistently to all applicants. Thus, a competitive examination may cause you some uneasiness now, but it is your privilege and safeguard.

C. HOW ARE CIVIL SERVICE EXAMS DEVELOPED?

Examinations are carefully written by trained technicians who are specialists in the field known as "psychological measurement," in consultation with recognized authorities in the field of work that the test will cover. These experts recommend the subject matter areas or skills to be tested; only those knowledges or skills important to your success on the job are included. The most reliable books and source materials available are used as references. Together, the experts and technicians judge the difficulty level of the questions.

Test technicians know how to phrase questions so that the problem is clearly stated. Their ethics do not permit "trick" or "catch" questions. Questions may have been tried out on sample groups, or subjected to statistical analysis, to determine their usefulness.

Written tests are often used in combination with performance tests, ratings of training and experience, and oral interviews. All of these measures combine to form the best-known means of finding the right person for the right job.

II. HOW TO PASS THE WRITTEN TEST

A. NATURE OF THE EXAMINATION

To prepare intelligently for civil service examinations, you should know how they differ from school examinations you have taken. In school you were assigned certain definite pages to read or subjects to cover. The examination questions were quite detailed and usually emphasized memory. Civil service exams, on the other hand, try to discover your present ability to perform the duties of a position, plus your potentiality to learn these duties. In other words, a civil service exam attempts to predict how successful you will be. Questions cover such a broad area that they cannot be as minute and detailed as school exam questions.

In the public service similar kinds of work, or positions, are grouped together in one "class." This process is known as *position-classification*. All the positions in a class are paid according to the salary range for that class. One class title covers all of these positions, and they are all tested by the same examination.

B. FOUR BASIC STEPS

1) Study the announcement

How, then, can you know what subjects to study? Our best answer is: "Learn as much as possible about the class of positions for which you've applied." The exam will test the knowledge, skills and abilities needed to do the work.

Your most valuable source of information about the position you want is the official exam announcement. This announcement lists the training and experience qualifications. Check these standards and apply only if you come reasonably close to meeting them.

The brief description of the position in the examination announcement offers some clues to the subjects which will be tested. Think about the job itself. Review the duties in your mind. Can you perform them, or are there some in which you are rusty? Fill in the blank spots in your preparation.

Many jurisdictions preview the written test in the exam announcement by including a section called "Knowledge and Abilities Required," "Scope of the Examination," or some similar heading. Here you will find out specifically what fields will be tested.

2) Review your own background

Once you learn in general what the position is all about, and what you need to know to do the work, ask yourself which subjects you already know fairly well and which need improvement. You may wonder whether to concentrate on improving your strong areas or on building some background in your fields of weakness. When the announcement has specified "some knowledge" or "considerable knowledge," or has used adjectives like "beginning principles of…" or "advanced … methods," you can get a clue as to the number and difficulty of questions to be asked in any given field. More questions, and hence broader coverage, would be included for those subjects which are more important in the work. Now weigh your strengths and weaknesses against the job requirements and prepare accordingly.

3) Determine the level of the position

Another way to tell how intensively you should prepare is to understand the level of the job for which you are applying. Is it the entering level? In other words, is this the position in which beginners in a field of work are hired? Or is it an intermediate or advanced level? Sometimes this is indicated by such words as "Junior" or "Senior" in the class title. Other jurisdictions use Roman numerals to designate the level – Clerk I, Clerk II, for example. The word "Supervisor" sometimes appears in the title. If the level is not indicated by the title, check the description of duties. Will you be working under very close supervision, or will you have responsibility for independent decisions in this work?

4) Choose appropriate study materials

Now that you know the subjects to be examined and the relative amount of each subject to be covered, you can choose suitable study materials. For beginning level jobs, or even advanced ones, if you have a pronounced weakness in some aspect of your training, read a modern, standard textbook in that field. Be sure it is up to date and has general coverage. Such books are normally available at your library, and the librarian will be glad to help you locate one. For entry-level positions, questions of appropriate difficulty are chosen – neither highly advanced questions, nor those too simple. Such questions require careful thought but not advanced training.

If the position for which you are applying is technical or advanced, you will read more advanced, specialized material. If you are already familiar with the basic principles of your field, elementary textbooks would waste your time. Concentrate on advanced textbooks and technical periodicals. Think through the concepts and review difficult problems in your field.

These are all general sources. You can get more ideas on your own initiative, following these leads. For example, training manuals and publications of the government agency which employs workers in your field can be useful, particularly for technical and professional positions. A letter or visit to the government department involved may result in more specific study suggestions, and certainly will provide you with a more definite idea of the exact nature of the position you are seeking.

III. KINDS OF TESTS

Tests are used for purposes other than measuring knowledge and ability to perform specified duties. For some positions, it is equally important to test ability to make adjustments to new situations or to profit from training. In others, basic mental abilities not dependent on information are essential. Questions which test these things may not appear as pertinent to the duties of the position as those which test for knowledge and information. Yet they are often highly important parts of a fair examination. For very general questions, it is almost impossible to help you direct your study efforts. What we can do is to point out some of the more common of these general abilities needed in public service positions and describe some typical questions.

1) General information

Broad, general information has been found useful for predicting job success in some kinds of work. This is tested in a variety of ways, from vocabulary lists to questions about current events. Basic background in some field of work, such as sociology or economics, may be sampled in a group of questions. Often these are principles which have become familiar to most persons through exposure rather than through formal training. It is difficult to advise you how to study for these questions; being alert to the world around you is our best suggestion.

2) Verbal ability

An example of an ability needed in many positions is verbal or language ability. Verbal ability is, in brief, the ability to use and understand words. Vocabulary and grammar tests are typical measures of this ability. Reading comprehension or paragraph interpretation questions are common in many kinds of civil service tests. You are given a paragraph of written material and asked to find its central meaning.

3) Numerical ability

Number skills can be tested by the familiar arithmetic problem, by checking paired lists of numbers to see which are alike and which are different, or by interpreting charts and graphs. In the latter test, a graph may be printed in the test booklet which you are asked to use as the basis for answering questions.

4) Observation

A popular test for law-enforcement positions is the observation test. A picture is shown to you for several minutes, then taken away. Questions about the picture test your ability to observe both details and larger elements.

5) Following directions

In many positions in the public service, the employee must be able to carry out written instructions dependably and accurately. You may be given a chart with several columns, each column listing a variety of information. The questions require you to carry out directions involving the information given in the chart.

6) Skills and aptitudes

Performance tests effectively measure some manual skills and aptitudes. When the skill is one in which you are trained, such as typing or shorthand, you can practice. These tests are often very much like those given in business school or high school - courses. For many of the other skills and aptitudes, however, no short-time preparation can be made. Skills and abilities natural to you or that you have developed throughout your lifetime are being tested.

Many of the general questions just described provide all the data needed to answer the questions and ask you to use your reasoning ability to find the answers. Your best preparation for these tests, as well as for tests of facts and ideas, is to be at your physical and mental best. You, no doubt, have your own methods of getting into an exam-taking mood and keeping "in shape." The next section lists some ideas on this subject.

IV. KINDS OF QUESTIONS

Only rarely is the "essay" question, which you answer in narrative form, used in civil service tests. Civil service tests are usually of the short-answer type. Full instructions for answering these questions will be given to you at the examination. But in case this is your first experience with short-answer questions and separate answer sheets, here is what you need to know:

1) Multiple-choice Questions

Most popular of the short-answer questions is the "multiple choice" or "best answer" question. It can be used, for example, to test for factual knowledge, ability to solve problems or judgment in meeting situations found at work.

A multiple-choice question is normally one of three types—

- It can begin with an incomplete statement followed by several possible endings. You are to find the one ending which *best* completes the statement, although some of the others may not be entirely wrong.
- It can also be a complete statement in the form of a question which is answered by choosing one of the statements listed.
- It can be in the form of a problem – again you select the best answer.

Here is an example of a multiple-choice question with a discussion which should give you some clues as to the method for choosing the right answer:

When an employee has a complaint about his assignment, the action which will *best* help him overcome his difficulty is to
  A. discuss his difficulty with his coworkers
  B. take the problem to the head of the organization
  C. take the problem to the person who gave him the assignment
  D. say nothing to anyone about his complaint

In answering this question, you should study each of the choices to find which is best. Consider choice "A" – Certainly an employee may discuss his complaint with fellow employees, but no change or improvement can result, and the complaint remains unresolved. Choice "B" is a poor choice since the head of the organization probably does not know what assignment you have been given, and taking your problem to him is known as "going over the head" of the supervisor. The supervisor, or person who made the assignment, is the person who can clarify it or correct any injustice. Choice "C" is, therefore, correct. To say nothing, as in choice "D," is unwise. Supervisors have and interest in knowing the problems employees are facing, and the employee is seeking a solution to his problem.

2) True/False Questions

The "true/false" or "right/wrong" form of question is sometimes used. Here a complete statement is given. Your job is to decide whether the statement is right or wrong.

SAMPLE: A person-to-person long-distance telephone call costs less than a station-to-station call to the same city.

This statement is wrong, or false, since person-to-person calls are more expensive.

This is not a complete list of all possible question forms, although most of the others are variations of these common types. You will always get complete directions for answering questions. Be sure you understand *how* to mark your answers – ask questions until you do.

V. RECORDING YOUR ANSWERS

For an examination with very few applicants, you may be told to record your answers in the test booklet itself. Separate answer sheets are much more common. If this separate answer sheet is to be scored by machine – and this is often the case – it is highly important that you mark your answers correctly in order to get credit.

An electric scoring machine is often used in civil service offices because of the speed with which papers can be scored. Machine-scored answer sheets must be marked with a pencil, which will be given to you. This pencil has a high graphite content which responds to the electric scoring machine. As a matter of fact, stray dots may register as answers, so do not let your pencil rest on the answer sheet while you are pondering the correct answer. Also, if your pencil lead breaks or is otherwise defective, ask for another.

Since the answer sheet will be dropped in a slot in the scoring machine, be careful not to bend the corners or get the paper crumpled.

The answer sheet normally has five vertical columns of numbers, with 30 numbers to a column. These numbers correspond to the question numbers in your test booklet. After each number, going across the page are four or five pairs of dotted lines. These short dotted lines have small letters or numbers above them. The first two pairs may also have a "T" or "F" above the letters. This indicates that the first two pairs only are to be used if the questions are of the true-false type. If the questions are multiple choice, disregard the "T" and "F" and pay attention only to the small letters or numbers.

Answer your questions in the manner of the sample that follows:

> 32. The largest city in the United States is
>   A. Washington, D.C.
>   B. New York City
>   C. Chicago
>   D. Detroit
>   E. San Francisco

1) Choose the answer you think is best. (New York City is the largest, so "B" is correct.)
2) Find the row of dotted lines numbered the same as the question you are answering. (Find row number 32)
3) Find the pair of dotted lines corresponding to the answer. (Find the pair of lines under the mark "B.")
4) Make a solid black mark between the dotted lines.

VI. BEFORE THE TEST

Common sense will help you find procedures to follow to get ready for an examination. Too many of us, however, overlook these sensible measures. Indeed, nervousness and fatigue have been found to be the most serious reasons why applicants fail to do their best on civil service tests. Here is a list of reminders:

- Begin your preparation early – Don't wait until the last minute to go scurrying around for books and materials or to find out what the position is all about.
- Prepare continuously – An hour a night for a week is better than an all-night cram session. This has been definitely established. What is more, a night a

6

week for a month will return better dividends than crowding your study into a shorter period of time.

- Locate the place of the exam – You have been sent a notice telling you when and where to report for the examination. If the location is in a different town or otherwise unfamiliar to you, it would be well to inquire the best route and learn something about the building.
- Relax the night before the test – Allow your mind to rest. Do not study at all that night. Plan some mild recreation or diversion; then go to bed early and get a good night's sleep.
- Get up early enough to make a leisurely trip to the place for the test – This way unforeseen events, traffic snarls, unfamiliar buildings, etc. will not upset you.
- Dress comfortably – A written test is not a fashion show. You will be known by number and not by name, so wear something comfortable.
- Leave excess paraphernalia at home – Shopping bags and odd bundles will get in your way. You need bring only the items mentioned in the official notice you received; usually everything you need is provided. Do not bring reference books to the exam. They will only confuse those last minutes and be taken away from you when in the test room.
- Arrive somewhat ahead of time – If because of transportation schedules you must get there very early, bring a newspaper or magazine to take your mind off yourself while waiting.
- Locate the examination room – When you have found the proper room, you will be directed to the seat or part of the room where you will sit. Sometimes you are given a sheet of instructions to read while you are waiting. Do not fill out any forms until you are told to do so; just read them and be prepared.
- Relax and prepare to listen to the instructions
- If you have any physical problem that may keep you from doing your best, be sure to tell the test administrator. If you are sick or in poor health, you really cannot do your best on the exam. You can come back and take the test some other time.

VII. AT THE TEST

The day of the test is here and you have the test booklet in your hand. The temptation to get going is very strong. Caution! There is more to success than knowing the right answers. You must know how to identify your papers and understand variations in the type of short-answer question used in this particular examination. Follow these suggestions for maximum results from your efforts:

1) Cooperate with the monitor

The test administrator has a duty to create a situation in which you can be as much at ease as possible. He will give instructions, tell you when to begin, check to see that you are marking your answer sheet correctly, and so on. He is not there to guard you, although he will see that your competitors do not take unfair advantage. He wants to help you do your best.

2) Listen to all instructions

Don't jump the gun! Wait until you understand all directions. In most civil service tests you get more time than you need to answer the questions. So don't be in a hurry.

Read each word of instructions until you clearly understand the meaning. Study the examples, listen to all announcements and follow directions. Ask questions if you do not understand what to do.

3) Identify your papers

Civil service exams are usually identified by number only. You will be assigned a number; you must not put your name on your test papers. Be sure to copy your number correctly. Since more than one exam may be given, copy your exact examination title.

4) Plan your time

Unless you are told that a test is a "speed" or "rate of work" test, speed itself is usually not important. Time enough to answer all the questions will be provided, but this does not mean that you have all day. An overall time limit has been set. Divide the total time (in minutes) by the number of questions to determine the approximate time you have for each question.

5) Do not linger over difficult questions

If you come across a difficult question, mark it with a paper clip (useful to have along) and come back to it when you have been through the booklet. One caution if you do this – be sure to skip a number on your answer sheet as well. Check often to be sure that you have not lost your place and that you are marking in the row numbered the same as the question you are answering.

6) Read the questions

Be sure you know what the question asks! Many capable people are unsuccessful because they failed to *read* the questions correctly.

7) Answer all questions

Unless you have been instructed that a penalty will be deducted for incorrect answers, it is better to guess than to omit a question.

8) Speed tests

It is often better NOT to guess on speed tests. It has been found that on timed tests people are tempted to spend the last few seconds before time is called in marking answers at random – without even reading them – in the hope of picking up a few extra points. To discourage this practice, the instructions may warn you that your score will be "corrected" for guessing. That is, a penalty will be applied. The incorrect answers will be deducted from the correct ones, or some other penalty formula will be used.

9) Review your answers

If you finish before time is called, go back to the questions you guessed or omitted to give them further thought. Review other answers if you have time.

10) Return your test materials

If you are ready to leave before others have finished or time is called, take ALL your materials to the monitor and leave quietly. Never take any test material with you. The monitor can discover whose papers are not complete, and taking a test booklet may be grounds for disqualification.

VIII. EXAMINATION TECHNIQUES

1) Read the general instructions carefully. These are usually printed on the first page of the exam booklet. As a rule, these instructions refer to the timing of the examination; the fact that you should not start work until the signal and must stop work at a signal, etc. If there are any *special* instructions, such as a choice of questions to be answered, make sure that you note this instruction carefully.

2) When you are ready to start work on the examination, that is as soon as the signal has been given, read the instructions to each question booklet, underline any key words or phrases, such as *least, best, outline, describe* and the like. In this way you will tend to answer as requested rather than discover on reviewing your paper that you *listed without describing*, that you selected the *worst* choice rather than the *best* choice, etc.

3) If the examination is of the objective or multiple-choice type – that is, each question will also give a series of possible answers: A, B, C or D, and you are called upon to select the best answer and write the letter next to that answer on your answer paper – it is advisable to start answering each question in turn. There may be anywhere from 50 to 100 such questions in the three or four hours allotted and you can see how much time would be taken if you read through all the questions before beginning to answer any. Furthermore, if you come across a question or group of questions which you know would be difficult to answer, it would undoubtedly affect your handling of all the other questions.

4) If the examination is of the essay type and contains but a few questions, it is a moot point as to whether you should read all the questions before starting to answer any one. Of course, if you are given a choice – say five out of seven and the like – then it is essential to read all the questions so you can eliminate the two that are most difficult. If, however, you are asked to answer all the questions, there may be danger in trying to answer the easiest one first because you may find that you will spend too much time on it. The best technique is to answer the first question, then proceed to the second, etc.

5) Time your answers. Before the exam begins, write down the time it started, then add the time allowed for the examination and write down the time it must be completed, then divide the time available somewhat as follows:
   - If 3-1/2 hours are allowed, that would be 210 minutes. If you have 80 objective-type questions, that would be an average of 2-1/2 minutes per question. Allow yourself no more than 2 minutes per question, or a total of 160 minutes, which will permit about 50 minutes to review.
   - If for the time allotment of 210 minutes there are 7 essay questions to answer, that would average about 30 minutes a question. Give yourself only 25 minutes per question so that you have about 35 minutes to review.

6) The most important instruction is to *read each question* and make sure you know what is wanted. The second most important instruction is to *time yourself properly* so that you answer every question. The third most

important instruction is to *answer every question*. Guess if you have to but include something for each question. Remember that you will receive no credit for a blank and will probably receive some credit if you write something in answer to an essay question. If you guess a letter – say "B" for a multiple-choice question – you may have guessed right. If you leave a blank as an answer to a multiple-choice question, the examiners may respect your feelings but it will not add a point to your score. Some exams may penalize you for wrong answers, so in such cases *only*, you may not want to guess unless you have some basis for your answer.

7) Suggestions
   a. Objective-type questions
     1. Examine the question booklet for proper sequence of pages and questions
     2. Read all instructions carefully
     3. Skip any question which seems too difficult; return to it after all other questions have been answered
     4. Apportion your time properly; do not spend too much time on any single question or group of questions
     5. Note and underline key words – *all, most, fewest, least, best, worst, same, opposite,* etc.
     6. Pay particular attention to negatives
     7. Note unusual option, e.g., unduly long, short, complex, different or similar in content to the body of the question
     8. Observe the use of "hedging" words – *probably, may, most likely,* etc.
     9. Make sure that your answer is put next to the same number as the question
     10. Do not second-guess unless you have good reason to believe the second answer is definitely more correct
     11. Cross out original answer if you decide another answer is more accurate; do not erase until you are ready to hand your paper in
     12. Answer all questions; guess unless instructed otherwise
     13. Leave time for review

   b. Essay questions
     1. Read each question carefully
     2. Determine exactly what is wanted. Underline key words or phrases.
     3. Decide on outline or paragraph answer
     4. Include many different points and elements unless asked to develop any one or two points or elements
     5. Show impartiality by giving pros and cons unless directed to select one side only
     6. Make and write down any assumptions you find necessary to answer the questions
     7. Watch your English, grammar, punctuation and choice of words
     8. Time your answers; don't crowd material

8) Answering the essay question

Most essay questions can be answered by framing the specific response around several key words or ideas. Here are a few such key words or ideas:

M's: manpower, materials, methods, money, management
P's: purpose, program, policy, plan, procedure, practice, problems, pitfalls, personnel, public relations

a. Six basic steps in handling problems:
1. Preliminary plan and background development
2. Collect information, data and facts
3. Analyze and interpret information, data and facts
4. Analyze and develop solutions as well as make recommendations
5. Prepare report and sell recommendations
6. Install recommendations and follow up effectiveness

b. Pitfalls to avoid
1. *Taking things for granted* – A statement of the situation does not necessarily imply that each of the elements is necessarily true; for example, a complaint may be invalid and biased so that all that can be taken for granted is that a complaint has been registered
2. *Considering only one side of a situation* – Wherever possible, indicate several alternatives and then point out the reasons you selected the best one
3. *Failing to indicate follow up* – Whenever your answer indicates action on your part, make certain that you will take proper follow-up action to see how successful your recommendations, procedures or actions turn out to be
4. *Taking too long in answering any single question* – Remember to time your answers properly

IX. AFTER THE TEST

Scoring procedures differ in detail among civil service jurisdictions although the general principles are the same. Whether the papers are hand-scored or graded by machine we have described, they are nearly always graded by number. That is, the person who marks the paper knows only the number – never the name – of the applicant. Not until all the papers have been graded will they be matched with names. If other tests, such as training and experience or oral interview ratings have been given, scores will be combined. Different parts of the examination usually have different weights. For example, the written test might count 60 percent of the final grade, and a rating of training and experience 40 percent. In many jurisdictions, veterans will have a certain number of points added to their grades.

After the final grade has been determined, the names are placed in grade order and an eligible list is established. There are various methods for resolving ties between those who get the same final grade – probably the most common is to place first the name of the person whose application was received first. Job offers are made from the eligible list in the order the names appear on it. You will be notified of your grade and your rank as soon as all these computations have been made. This will be done as rapidly as possible.

People who are found to meet the requirements in the announcement are called "eligibles." Their names are put on a list of eligible candidates. An eligible's chances of getting a job depend on how high he stands on this list and how fast agencies are filling jobs from the list.

When a job is to be filled from a list of eligibles, the agency asks for the names of people on the list of eligibles for that job. When the civil service commission receives this request, it sends to the agency the names of the three people highest on this list. Or, if the job to be filled has specialized requirements, the office sends the agency the names of the top three persons who meet these requirements from the general list.

The appointing officer makes a choice from among the three people whose names were sent to him. If the selected person accepts the appointment, the names of the others are put back on the list to be considered for future openings.

That is the rule in hiring from all kinds of eligible lists, whether they are for typist, carpenter, chemist, or something else. For every vacancy, the appointing officer has his choice of any one of the top three eligibles on the list. This explains why the person whose name is on top of the list sometimes does not get an appointment when some of the persons lower on the list do. If the appointing officer chooses the second or third eligible, the No. 1 eligible does not get a job at once, but stays on the list until he is appointed or the list is terminated.

X. HOW TO PASS THE INTERVIEW TEST

The examination for which you applied requires an oral interview test. You have already taken the written test and you are now being called for the interview test – the final part of the formal examination.

You may think that it is not possible to prepare for an interview test and that there are no procedures to follow during an interview. Our purpose is to point out some things you can do in advance that will help you and some good rules to follow and pitfalls to avoid while you are being interviewed.

What is an interview supposed to test?

The written examination is designed to test the technical knowledge and competence of the candidate; the oral is designed to evaluate intangible qualities, not readily measured otherwise, and to establish a list showing the relative fitness of each candidate – as measured against his competitors – for the position sought. Scoring is not on the basis of "right" and "wrong," but on a sliding scale of values ranging from "not passable" to "outstanding." As a matter of fact, it is possible to achieve a relatively low score without a single "incorrect" answer because of evident weakness in the qualities being measured.

Occasionally, an examination may consist entirely of an oral test – either an individual or a group oral. In such cases, information is sought concerning the technical knowledges and abilities of the candidate, since there has been no written examination for this purpose. More commonly, however, an oral test is used to supplement a written examination.

Who conducts interviews?

The composition of oral boards varies among different jurisdictions. In nearly all, a representative of the personnel department serves as chairman. One of the members of the board may be a representative of the department in which the candidate would work. In some cases, "outside experts" are used, and, frequently, a businessman or some other representative of the general public is asked to serve. Labor and management or other special groups may be represented. The aim is to secure the services of experts in the appropriate field.

However the board is composed, it is a good idea (and not at all improper or unethical) to ascertain in advance of the interview who the members are and what groups they represent. When you are introduced to them, you will have some idea of their backgrounds and interests, and at least you will not stutter and stammer over their names.

What should be done before the interview?

While knowledge about the board members is useful and takes some of the surprise element out of the interview, there is other preparation which is more substantive. It *is* possible to prepare for an oral interview – in several ways:

1) Keep a copy of your application and review it carefully before the interview

This may be the only document before the oral board, and the starting point of the interview. Know what education and experience you have listed there, and the sequence and dates of all of it. Sometimes the board will ask you to review the highlights of your experience for them; you should not have to hem and haw doing it.

2) Study the class specification and the examination announcement

Usually, the oral board has one or both of these to guide them. The qualities, characteristics or knowledges required by the position sought are stated in these documents. They offer valuable clues as to the nature of the oral interview. For example, if the job involves supervisory responsibilities, the announcement will usually indicate that knowledge of modern supervisory methods and the qualifications of the candidate as a supervisor will be tested. If so, you can expect such questions, frequently in the form of a hypothetical situation which you are expected to solve. NEVER go into an oral without knowledge of the duties and responsibilities of the job you seek.

3) Think through each qualification required

Try to visualize the kind of questions you would ask if you were a board member. How well could you answer them? Try especially to appraise your own knowledge and background in each area, *measured against the job sought*, and identify any areas in which you are weak. Be critical and realistic – do not flatter yourself.

4) Do some general reading in areas in which you feel you may be weak

For example, if the job involves supervision and your past experience has NOT, some general reading in supervisory methods and practices, particularly in the field of human relations, might be useful. Do NOT study agency procedures or detailed manuals. The oral board will be testing your understanding and capacity, not your memory.

5) Get a good night's sleep and watch your general health and mental attitude

You will want a clear head at the interview. Take care of a cold or any other minor ailment, and of course, no hangovers.

What should be done on the day of the interview?

Now comes the day of the interview itself. Give yourself plenty of time to get there. Plan to arrive somewhat ahead of the scheduled time, particularly if your appointment is in the fore part of the day. If a previous candidate fails to appear, the board might be ready for you a bit early. By early afternoon an oral board is almost invariably behind schedule if there are many candidates, and you may have to wait.

Take along a book or magazine to read, or your application to review, but leave any extraneous material in the waiting room when you go in for your interview. In any event, relax and compose yourself.

The matter of dress is important. The board is forming impressions about you – from your experience, your manners, your attitude, and your appearance. Give your personal appearance careful attention. Dress your best, but not your flashiest. Choose conservative, appropriate clothing, and be sure it is immaculate. This is a business interview, and your appearance should indicate that you regard it as such. Besides, being well groomed and properly dressed will help boost your confidence.

Sooner or later, someone will call your name and escort you into the interview room. *This is it.* From here on you are on your own. It is too late for any more preparation. But remember, you asked for this opportunity to prove your fitness, and you are here because your request was granted.

What happens when you go in?

The usual sequence of events will be as follows: The clerk (who is often the board stenographer) will introduce you to the chairman of the oral board, who will introduce you to the other members of the board. Acknowledge the introductions before you sit down. Do not be surprised if you find a microphone facing you or a stenotypist sitting by. Oral interviews are usually recorded in the event of an appeal or other review.

Usually the chairman of the board will open the interview by reviewing the highlights of your education and work experience from your application – primarily for the benefit of the other members of the board, as well as to get the material into the record. Do not interrupt or comment unless there is an error or significant misinterpretation; if that is the case, do not hesitate. But do not quibble about insignificant matters. Also, he will usually ask you some question about your education, experience or your present job – partly to get you to start talking and to establish the interviewing "rapport." He may start the actual questioning, or turn it over to one of the other members. Frequently, each member undertakes the questioning on a particular area, one in which he is perhaps most competent, so you can expect each member to participate in the examination. Because time is limited, you may also expect some rather abrupt switches in the direction the questioning takes, so do not be upset by it. Normally, a board member will not pursue a single line of questioning unless he discovers a particular strength or weakness.

After each member has participated, the chairman will usually ask whether any member has any further questions, then will ask you if you have anything you wish to add. Unless you are expecting this question, it may floor you. Worse, it may start you off on an extended, extemporaneous speech. The board is not usually seeking more information. The question is principally to offer you a last opportunity to present further qualifications or to indicate that you have nothing to add. So, if you feel that a significant qualification or characteristic has been overlooked, it is proper to point it out in a sentence or so. Do not compliment the board on the thoroughness of their examination – they have been sketchy, and you know it. If you wish, merely say, "No thank you, I have nothing further to add." This is a point where you can "talk yourself out" of a good impression or fail to present an important bit of information. Remember, *you close the interview yourself.*

The chairman will then say, "That is all, Mr. _____, thank you." Do not be startled; the interview is over, and quicker than you think. Thank him, gather your belongings and take your leave. Save your sigh of relief for the other side of the door.

How to put your best foot forward

Throughout this entire process, you may feel that the board individually and collectively is trying to pierce your defenses, seek out your hidden weaknesses and embarrass and confuse you. Actually, this is not true. They are obliged to make an appraisal of your qualifications for the job you are seeking, and they want to see you in your best light. Remember, they must interview all candidates and a non-cooperative candidate may become a failure in spite of their best efforts to bring out his qualifications. Here are 15 suggestions that will help you:

1) Be natural – Keep your attitude confident, not cocky

If you are not confident that you can do the job, do not expect the board to be. Do not apologize for your weaknesses, try to bring out your strong points. The board is interested in a positive, not negative, presentation. Cockiness will antagonize any board member and make him wonder if you are covering up a weakness by a false show of strength.

2) Get comfortable, but don't lounge or sprawl

Sit erectly but not stiffly. A careless posture may lead the board to conclude that you are careless in other things, or at least that you are not impressed by the importance of the occasion. Either conclusion is natural, even if incorrect. Do not fuss with your clothing, a pencil or an ashtray. Your hands may occasionally be useful to emphasize a point; do not let them become a point of distraction.

3) Do not wisecrack or make small talk

This is a serious situation, and your attitude should show that you consider it as such. Further, the time of the board is limited – they do not want to waste it, and neither should you.

4) Do not exaggerate your experience or abilities

In the first place, from information in the application or other interviews and sources, the board may know more about you than you think. Secondly, you probably will not get away with it. An experienced board is rather adept at spotting such a situation, so do not take the chance.

5) If you know a board member, do not make a point of it, yet do not hide it

Certainly you are not fooling him, and probably not the other members of the board. Do not try to take advantage of your acquaintanceship – it will probably do you little good.

6) Do not dominate the interview

Let the board do that. They will give you the clues – do not assume that you have to do all the talking. Realize that the board has a number of questions to ask you, and do not try to take up all the interview time by showing off your extensive knowledge of the answer to the first one.

7) Be attentive

You only have 20 minutes or so, and you should keep your attention at its sharpest throughout. When a member is addressing a problem or question to you, give him your undivided attention. Address your reply principally to him, but do not exclude the other board members.

8) Do not interrupt

A board member may be stating a problem for you to analyze. He will ask you a question when the time comes. Let him state the problem, and wait for the question.

9) Make sure you understand the question

Do not try to answer until you are sure what the question is. If it is not clear, restate it in your own words or ask the board member to clarify it for you. However, do not haggle about minor elements.

10) Reply promptly but not hastily

A common entry on oral board rating sheets is "candidate responded readily," or "candidate hesitated in replies." Respond as promptly and quickly as you can, but do not jump to a hasty, ill-considered answer.

11) Do not be peremptory in your answers

A brief answer is proper – but do not fire your answer back. That is a losing game from your point of view. The board member can probably ask questions much faster than you can answer them.

12) Do not try to create the answer you think the board member wants

He is interested in what kind of mind you have and how it works – not in playing games. Furthermore, he can usually spot this practice and will actually grade you down on it.

13) Do not switch sides in your reply merely to agree with a board member

Frequently, a member will take a contrary position merely to draw you out and to see if you are willing and able to defend your point of view. Do not start a debate, yet do not surrender a good position. If a position is worth taking, it is worth defending.

14) Do not be afraid to admit an error in judgment if you are shown to be wrong

The board knows that you are forced to reply without any opportunity for careful consideration. Your answer may be demonstrably wrong. If so, admit it and get on with the interview.

15) Do not dwell at length on your present job

The opening question may relate to your present assignment. Answer the question but do not go into an extended discussion. You are being examined for a *new* job, not your present one. As a matter of fact, try to phrase ALL your answers in terms of the job for which you are being examined.

Basis of Rating

Probably you will forget most of these "do's" and "don'ts" when you walk into the oral interview room. Even remembering them all will not ensure you a passing grade. Perhaps you did not have the qualifications in the first place. But remembering them will help you to put your best foot forward, without treading on the toes of the board members.

Rumor and popular opinion to the contrary notwithstanding, an oral board wants you to make the best appearance possible. They know you are under pressure – but they also want to see how you respond to it as a guide to what your reaction would be under the pressures of the job you seek. They will be influenced by the degree of poise you display, the personal traits you show and the manner in which you respond.

EXAMINATION SECTION

EXAMINATION SECTION
TEST 1

DIRECTIONS: Each question or incomplete statement is followed by several suggested answers or completions. Select the one that BEST answers the question or completes the statement. *PRINT THE LETTER OF THE CORRECT ANSWER IN THE SPACE AT THE RIGHT.*

1. An indictment is a   1.____

    A. formal charge
    B. overdue payment
    C. bill of particulars relating to a dispute
    D. felony

2. In a trial, a hostile witness is a(n) _____ witness.   2.____

    A. controversial   B. unfriendly
    C. combative   D. evasive

3. Which of the following was an event from 1999 that may reduce the number of guns in this country?   3.____

    A. The passage of a strict gun law in Congress
    B. Gun shows were restricted by Congress
    C. The Colt Corporation restricted the sale of its guns
    D. An embargo was placed on guns coming into this country

4. In the state, headlights should be used when visibility is equal to a minimum or less than _____ feet. 4.____

    A. 500   B. 750   C. 1,000   D. 1,250

5. You are required to dim your headlights when an approaching vehicle is within _____ feet of your vehicle. 5.____

    A. 500   B. 400   C. 300   D. 200

6. *Some features of the arrangement of contents in the following pages may perplex some readers.*   6.____
The word *perplex*, as used in the above sentence, means MOST NEARLY

    A. interest   B. enlighten
    C. turnoff   D. confuse

7. Hearsay evidence means   7.____

    A. false evidence
    B. evidence that needs to be verified
    C. it is generally not admissible in court
    D. the person testifying is unsure of its truth

Questions 8-9.

DIRECTIONS: Questions 8 and 9 refer to the following paragraph.

The variations in report writing range from such picayune details as using A.M. or a.m. to more substantive issues as the inclusion or omission of a report summary in the first para-graph.

8.   In the above paragraph, the word *picayune* means MOST NEARLY   8.___

    A.   grammatic   B.   debatable
    C.   trivial   D.   tendentious

9.   In the above paragraph, the word *substantive* means MOST NEARLY   9.___

    A.   cursory   B.   meaningless
    C.   critical   D.   substantial

10.   In accordance with the driver's manual issued by the state, you must report an accident   10.___
when damage is _____ or more.

    A. $500   B. $1,000   C. $1,500   D. $2,000

11.   It is easier to pass a heavy truck on a highway   11.___

    A.   when the roadway is level
    B.   when going uphill
    C.   when going downhill
    D.   on a concrete pavement

12.   In most states, motorcyclists are required to use   12.___

    A.   headlights and taillights only after sundown
    B.   headlights and taillights at all times
    C.   taillights only during daylight hours
    D.   headlights only during daylight hours

13.   DNA refers to   13.___

    A.   a person who dies upon arriving at a hospital
    B.   genetic material
    C.   a chemical reaction
    D.   a powerful drug

14.   An odometer measures the _____ an automobile.   14.___

    A.   speed of
    B.   velocity of
    C.   distance traveled by
    D.   revolutions per second of the engine of

15.   *Profiling has recently become a controversial issue in police work.*   15.___
Profiling, as used in the above sentence, relates to paying special attention to

    A.   a recognizable class of people
    B.   people of low income

C. people who exceed the speed limits
D. the class of people who drive expensive cars

16. Most highways have a minimum speed of _____ MPH.   16._____

    A. 40   B. 35   C. 30   D. 25

17. The lowest automobile accident rate occurs in the _____ year age group.   17._____

    A. 20 to 35   B. 35 to 50   C. 50 to 65   D. 65 to 80

18. *Writing is characterized as narrative description, exposition, and argument.*   18._____
Exposition, as used in the above sentence, means MOST NEARLY

    A. describing the circumstances of the situation
    B. the explanation of a piece of information
    C. explaining your conclusions
    D. giving the pros and cons of a conclusion

19. A report states that the latent prints have been sent to the laboratory. The word *latent,* as   19._____
used in the above statement, means MOST NEARLY

    A. missing   B. visible   C. hidden   D. damaged

20. After being *acquitted* in the first trial, O.J. Simpson faced a second trial. The second trial   20._____
was not double jeopardy because

    A. evidence was withheld from the jury
    B. he was tried on different criminal charges
    C. the second trial was a civil trial
    D. the first trial was against the weight of the evidence

21. To *loiter* means MOST NEARLY to   21._____

    A. gather in a group of five or more
    B. create suspicion of wrongdoing while hanging around
    C. obstruct pedestrian movement
    D. linger in an aimless way

22. The minimum automobile insurance required for property damage in New York State is   22._____

    A. $3,000   B. $5,000   C. $10,000   D. $20,000

23. The maximum speed limit in a village or town is usually _____ MPH.   23._____

    A. 20   B. 25   C. 30   D. 40

24. The purpose of the *two second rule* in driving is to   24._____

    A. give you enough time to stop if there is a traffic signal ahead
    B. give you enough clearance to cut into another lane when passing a car
    C. keep enough room between your vehicle and the one ahead
    D. provide enough room when entering a highway

25. In most states, you may be arrested for driving with a blood alcohol content of _____   25.___
     percent or more.

    A. .05   B. .10   C. .15   D. .20

KEY (CORRECT ANSWERS)

1.	A		11.	B
2.	B		12.	B
3.	C		13.	B
4.	C		14.	C
5.	A		15.	A
6.	D		16.	A
7.	C		17.	B
8.	C		18.	B
9.	D		19.	C
10.	B		20.	C

21.	D
22.	B
23.	C
24.	C
25.	B

TEST 2

DIRECTIONS: Each question or incomplete statement is followed by several suggested answers or completions. Select the one that BEST answers the question or completes the statement. *PRINT THE LETTER OF THE CORRECT ANSWER IN THE SPACE AT THE RIGHT.*

1. A yellow sign showing two children in black indicates a school crossing. The shape of the sign is a

    A. square   B. rectangle   C. hexagon   D. pentagon

1.____

2. Personal vehicles driven by volunteer firefighters responding to alarms are allowed to display _____ lights.

    A. blue   B. green   C. red   D. amber

2.____

3. The color amber is closest to

    A. green   B. yellow   C. purple   D. blue

3.____

4. Larceny in the legal sense means

    A. the unlawful taking away of another person's property without his consent
    B. overcharging another person who is making a purchase
    C. deceiving another person as to the value of an item he wishes to purchase
    D. adding a service charge to an agreed price to an item that is purchased

4.____

5. A misdemeanor in law refers to

    A. a financial dispute between two litigants
    B. a minor offense
    C. a burglary where a small amount of goods was stolen
    D. unruly behavior in public

5.____

6. An overt act means MOST NEARLY a(n)

    A. foolish act   B. act done publicly
    C. illegal act   D. outrageous act

6.____

7. A defense lawyer works for a client *pro bono*. This means he

    A. gets paid only if he wins the case
    B. gets paid a fixed fee
    C. works for free
    D. represents his client at half his usual fee

7.____

8. Corpus delicti refers to the

    A. missing person   B. murderer
    C. scene of the crime   D. dead victim

8.____

9. The shape of a stop sign is

    A. triangular   B. square
    C. six-sided   D. eight-sided

9.____

10. Service signs are _____ with white letters and symbols.   10.___

    A. blue   B. green   C. yellow   D. red

11. Destination signs are _____ with white letters and symbols.   11.___

    A. blue   B. green   C. yellow   D. red

12. According to the driver's manual, you are prohibited from passing if you cannot safely   12.___
    return to the right lane before any approaching vehicle comes within _____ feet of your
    car.

    A. 100   B. 150   C. 200   D. 250

13. When parking near a hydrant, you must be clear of the hydrant a minimum distance of   13.___
    _____ feet.

    A. 5   B. 10   C. 15   D. 20

14. When parking your vehicle between two parked vehicles, you must park a maximum of   14.___
    _____ inches from the curb.

    A. 12   B. 15   C. 18   D. 21

15. In order to insure approval, the framers of the Constitution agreed to add a series of   15.___
    amendments after approval to protect people's rights.
    The number of amendments that were added is

    A. six   B. eight   C. ten   D. twelve

16. The amendment number that insures a person's right to bear arms is   16.___

    A. one   B. two   C. three   D. five

17. The amendment number that prevents a person from incriminating himself is   17.___

    A. one   B. three   C. five   D. seven

18. The right of a person to be secure in his house, and against unreasonable search is   18.___
    amendment number

    A. two   B. four   C. six   D. eight

19. The right of people to assemble peaceably is amendment number   19.___

    A. one   B. two   C. three   D. four

20. 90 kilometers per hour is equivalent to _____ MPH.   20.___

    A. 40   B. 45   C. 50   D. 55

21. A commercial driver's license is required if the vehicle being driven has a gross weight   21.___
    rating of equal to or more than _____ pounds.

    A. 24,000   B. 26,000   C. 28,000   D. 30,000

22. One kilogram is equivalent to _____ pounds.   22.___

    A. 2.2   B. 2.4   C. 2.6   D. 2.8

23. Failing to stop for a school bus in New York State is worth _____ points on your license.   23.____

    A. 3   B. 4   C. 5   D. 6

24. In the state, the minimum liability insurance required against the death of one person is   24.____

    A. $30,000   B. $50,000   C. $100,000   D. $150,000

25. Before a person is arrested, he is read a statement by the arresting officer. The name   25.____
associated with this procedure is

    A. Megan   B. Zenger   C. Scott   D. Miranda

KEY (CORRECT ANSWERS)

1.	D		11.	B
2.	A		12.	C
3.	B		13.	C
4.	A		14.	A
5.	B		15.	C
6.	B		16.	B
7.	C		17.	C
8.	D		18.	B
9.	D		19.	A
10.	A		20.	D

21.	B
22.	A
23.	C
24.	B
25.	D

TEST 3

DIRECTIONS: Each question or incomplete statement is followed by several suggested answers or completions. Select the one that BEST answers the question or completes the statement. *PRINT THE LETTER OF THE CORRECT ANSWER IN THE SPACE AT THE RIGHT.*

1. In legal terms, a deposition is   1.____

    A.   a statement made by a person in open court
    B.   a statement under oath, but not in open court
    C.   the testimony made by a defendant under oath in open court
    D.   a statement under oath that is mainly hearsay

2. In an automobile accident, first check to see if the injured person is breathing. If not,   2.____
    apply

    A.   MPR   B.   IBR   C.   FHR   D.   CPR

3. Hazard vehicles, such as snow plows and tow trucks, display _____ -colored lights.   3.____

    A.   blue   B.   green   C.   amber   D.   red

4. The hand signal shown at the right indicates   4.____
    A.   caution because there is an obstruction ahead
    B.   a right turn
    C.   a left turn
    D.   a stop

5. A felony is a   5.____

    A.   crime only where someone is murdered
    B.   major crime
    C.   crime only where someone is injured
    D.   crime only where major physical damage occurs

6. *Embezzlement* means MOST NEARLY   6.____

    A.   deceiving   B.   the hiding of funds
    C.   stealing   D.   investing illegally

7. The writer should be wary of using an entire paragraph for information, while necessary   7.___
    is not really of great importance.
    The word *wary* in the above sentence means MOST NEARLY

    A.   uncertain   B.   cautious
    C.   certain   D.   serious

8. Hearsay evidence is evidence that   8.____

    A.   is usually admissible in court
    B.   can be inferred from preceding evidence
    C.   is based on what another person said out of court
    D.   is implied in the testimony of a witness

9. *Excessive bail shall not be required* is amendment number   9.____

    A. two   B. four   C. six   D. eight

10. The writ of habeas corpus is used to   10.____

    A. insure a defendant receives a fair trial
    B. insure a defendant's Fifth Amendment rights
    C. reduce or eliminate bail
    D. prevent a person from being detained illegally

11. The number of justices in the United States Supreme Court is   11.____

    A. 6   B. 7   C. 8   D. 9

12. The *blue wall* refers to law enforcement officers who   12.____

    A. do not publicly condemn fellow officers regardless of facts
    B. set up roadblocks
    C. support their superiors
    D. do their utmost to improve their image

13. The difference between burglary and robbery is   13.____

    A. burglary is breaking into a building to commit theft, while robbery is the use of vio-
        lence in taking property from a person
    B. the money value taken in a burglary is less than $10,000, whereas in a robbery the
        money value taken is more than $10,000
    C. burglary takes place at night, whereas robbery takes place in the daytime
    D. burglary takes place indoors, whereas robbery takes place outdoors

14. The Federal government announced new guidelines relating to automobiles. These stan-   14.____
dards relate to

    A. automobile weight   B. gas mileage requirements
    C. car infant seats   D. bumper heights

15. General Motors was involved in a famous lawsuit relating to the Chevy Corvair based on   15.____

    A. its crashworthiness
    B. faulty design of the brake system
    C. failure of the transmissions
    D. location of the gas tanks

16. State legislatures are considering restrictions on the use of cellular phones while driving   16.____
an automobile. The main argument for the restrictions is that

    A. driving with one hand is hazardous
    B. conversations on the phone are a distraction
    C. cellular phones interfere with the ignition system
    D. the driver is unlikely to hear sirens or hornblowing

17. *Much of their business involves the unpredictable and the bizarre.*   17.____
The word *bizarre*, as used in the above statement, means MOST NEARLY

    A. weird   B. routine
    C. complicated   D. life-threatening

18. *The federal government seized 145 metric tons of cocaine coming into the United States from South America.*
    A metric ton is equal to _____ pounds.

    A. 1,800   B. 2,000   C. 2,200   D. 2,400

18.___

19. A kilogram is most nearly _____ pounds.

    A. 2.0   B. 2.2   C. 2.4   D. 2.6

19.___

20. A narcotic drug used in medicine, but less habit-forming than morphine, is

    A. cocaine   B. methadone   C. LSD   D. heroin

20.___

21. Of the following, the one that is a hazard for the large recreational vehicles is

    A. their inability to meet the emission requirements
    B. their bumper height above the ground does not match the height of the bumpers on the smaller-sized vehicles
    C. because the driver is high above the ground, his ability to see his surroundings is impaired
    D. because of the high center of gravity of the recreational vehicles, they become unstable at high speeds

21.___

22. State inspection procedures on emissions focus on

    A. hydrocarbons and CO_2 B. CO and CO_2
    C. SO_2 and CO   D. hydrocarbons and CO

22.___

23. *In order to bring a case before a Grand Jury, the prosecutor must present a prima facie case of guilt before the Grand Jury.*
    Prima facie in the above statement means MOST NEARLY

    A. overwhelming evidence to convict
    B. sufficient to convict unless rebutted by the defense
    C. possibly sufficient to convict by an objective jury
    D. with additional evidence would be sufficient to convict

23.___

24. The KKK was denied a permit to hold a parade in New York City. The Klan sued in court claiming a violation of their rights under the _____ Amendment.

    A. First   B. Third   C. Fifth   D. Eighth

24.___

25. In a jury trial for a felony, a jury of twelve must have

    A. a majority decision
    B. 9 members finding the defendant guilty
    C. 11 members finding the defendant guilty
    D. a unanimous finding of guilt

25.___

KEY (CORRECT ANSWERS)

1.	B		11.	D
2.	D		12.	A
3.	C		13.	A
4.	D		14.	C
5.	B		15.	D
6.	C		16.	B
7.	B		17.	A
8.	C		18.	C
9.	D		19.	B
10.	D		20.	B

21.	B
22.	D
23.	B
24.	A
25.	D

———

TEST 4

DIRECTIONS: Each question or incomplete statement is followed by several suggested answers or completions. Select the one that BEST answers the question or completes the statement. *PRINT THE LETTER OF THE CORRECT ANSWER IN THE SPACE AT THE RIGHT.*

1. State law defines a juvenile as _____ years of age or less.   1.___

    A.   15   B.   16   C.   17   D.   18

2. A writ of habeas corpus is an order to   2.___

    A.   dismiss charges against a detained person
    B.   reduce the charges against a detained person
    C.   have a detained person confront his accusors
    D.   have a detained person brought before a court

3. A person is brought into a police station to face charges. The person brought in when interrogated refuses to tell more than his name and address.
In the face of his silence, the proper course to be followed by the interviewer is to   3.___

    A.   remind the detainee that he is guilty of obstruction of justice
    B.   stop the interrogation
    C.   remind the detainee that his unwillingness to cooperate will result in high bail
    D.   tell the interviewee he is required to cooperate with the police

4. *The implication in most discussions on police discretion is that it is the police administrator who should undertake to spell out policies and rules.*
In the above statement, the word *discretion* means MOST NEARLY   4.___

    A.   the power to judge or act
    B.   behavior
    C.   competence
    D.   ability to reach a conclusion

5. A nickname for amphetamine is   5.___

    A.   ice   B.   pot   C.   downer   D.   grass

6. A nickname for cocaine is   6.___

    A.   speed   B.   red devils
    C.   snow   D.   Mary Jane

7. A nickname for marijuana is   7.___

    A.   ice   B.   downer   C.   snow   D.   grass

8. A nickname for barbiturates is   8.___

    A.   angel dust   B.   quaaludes
    C.   meth   D.   downers

9. Of the following, the most widely used drug is   9.____

    A. LSD   B. crack   C. marijuana   D. cocaine

10. Crack is related to   10.____

    A. angel dust   B. quaaludes
    C. LSD   D. cocaine

11. The police department is changing the type of ammunition they use. The new bullets will   11.____
have a softer head. The main reason for this change is that

    A. it will not ricochet if it hits a wall
    B. it will cause less injury to a person struck by the bullet
    C. the bullet is less expensive
    D. it will be easier to recover

12. Of the following weapons, the one that is of the semiautomatic type is the   12.____

    A. Colt revolver   B. 45
    C. AK-47   D. Springfield rifle

13. A *Saturday Night Special* is a   13.____

    A. semi-automatic gun   B. small, cheaply made weapon
    C. gun used for hunting   D. difficult gun to conceal

14. One inch is equal to _____ centimeters.   14.____

    A. 2.54   B. 2.64   C. 2.74   D. 2.84

15. A gun control bill was passed in Congress that was named after President Reagan's   15.____
press secretary who was shot in an attack on the President. The name of the bill was the
_____ bill.

    A. McClure   B. Brady
    C. Volkmer   D. Everett Koop

16. In New York City, if you are caught carrying a concealed gun for which you do not have a   16.____
permit, you can be jailed for a maximum of _____ months.

    A. 3   B. 6   C. 9   D. 12

17. The Federal Firearm License Law is designed to ensure that individuals who obtain   17.____
licenses have a legitimate reason for doing so and to deny guns to

    A. people who carry large amounts of money on their person
    B. people who have a criminal record
    C. senior citizens
    D. people under 22 years old

18. According to government studies, the number of guns in the United States is over   18.____
_____ million.

    A. one hundred   B. one hundred and twenty
    C. one hundred and fifty   D. two hundred

19. According to statistics, when a woman is killed with a gun, it is LEAST likely to be by   19.____

A. her husband   B. a relative
C. a stranger   D. a friend

20. Federal law states that a person is prohibited from buying a gun who is under the age of   20.___

    A. sixteen   B. eighteen
    C. twenty   D. twenty-two

21. Of the following countries in South America, the one that is the largest exporter of drugs   21.___
into the United States is

    A. Columbia   B. Venezuela
    C. Chile   D. Argentina

22. Of the following, the state in the United States that allows citizens to carry concealed   22.___
guns is

    A. Arizona   B. New Mexico
    C. Texas   D. Oklahoma

23. A bullet has a diameter of 9 mm. Its diameter, in inches, is MOST NEARLY _____ inch.   23.___

    A. 1/4   B. 3/8   C. 1/2   D. 5/8

24. The repeal of the amendment to the Constitution barring the manufacture and selling of   24.___
whiskey occurred under the administration of President

    A. Roosevelt   B. Hoover   C. Truman   D. Coolidge

25. The shrub from which cocaine is derived is   25.___

    A. cacao   B. hemp   C. liana   D. coca

KEY (CORRECT ANSWERS)

1.	D		11.	A
2.	D		12.	C
3.	B		13.	B
4.	A		14.	A
5.	A		15.	B
6.	C		16.	D
7.	D		17.	B
8.	D		18.	D
9.	C		19.	C
10.	D		20.	B

21.	A
22.	C
23.	B
24.	A
25.	D

EXAMINATION SECTION
TEST 1

DIRECTIONS: Each question or incomplete statement is followed by several suggested answers or completions. Select the one the BEST answers the question or completes the statement. *PRINT THE LETTER OF THE CORRECT ANSWER IN THE SPACE AT THE RIGHT.*

1. Officer Hayes has arrived at the scene of an automobile accident to find the two drivers arguing heatedly in the middle of the intersection, where their two cars remain entangled by their front bumpers. Traffic has backed up on all four sides of the intersection. As Officer Hayes approaches, the two drivers each begin to tell their side of the story at the same time. As they grow more agitated and begin to call each other names, one of the drivers threatens the other with physical harm. In this situation, Officer Hayes' first action should be to

    A. ask each driver to stand on an opposite corner of the intersection and wait for him to begin documenting the accident
    B. call a tow truck to clear the accident from the intersection
    C. arrest the driver who made the threat
    D. ask the drivers to pull their cars out of the intersection and off to the side of the road

1.____

2. Probably the most important thing a police officer can do to build and strengthen a trusting relationship with community members is to

    A. patrol the area often and conspicuously
    B. listen to them in a respectful and nonjudgemental way
    C. make sure people understand his background and qualifications
    D. establish clear, reachable goals for improving the community

2.____

3. Which of the following is NOT a factor that should influence an officer's exercise of discretion?

    A. Clear statutes and protocols
    B. Informal expectations of legislatures and the public
    C. Use of force
    D. Limited resources

3.____

4. The term for the policing style which emphasizes order maintenance is _____ style.

    A. service
    B. coercive
    C. watchman
    D. legalistic

4.____

5. Officer Torres, a community service law enforcement officer, approaches the home of recent Vietnamese immigrants to speak to several community members gathered there. He notices several pairs of shoes on the front porch. It is reasonable for Officer Torres to assume that

    A. the people in the home are superstitious
    B. the house must have some religious significance

5.____

C. if he removes his own shoes before entering, it will be perceived as a sign of respect
D. the homeowners are having their carpets cleaned

6. Ethical issues are

6.___

A. usually a problem only in individual behaviors
B. relevant to all aspects of police work
C. usually referred to a board or committee for decision-making
D. the same as legal issues

7. In using the "reflection of meaning" technique in a client interview, a social worker should do each of the following, EXCEPT

7.___

A. Begin with a sentence stem such as "You mean..." or "Sounds like you believe..."
B. Offer an interpretation of the client's words.
C. Add paraphrasing of longer client statements.
D. Close with a "check-out" such as, "Am I hearing you right?"

8. A police officer is speaking with a victim who is hearing-impaired. The police officer should try to do each of the following, EXCEPT

8.___

A. speak slowly and clearly
B. gradually increase the volume of his voice
C. face the victim squarely
D. reduce or eliminate any background or ambient noise

9. An officer is interviewing a witness who is a recent immigrant from China. In general, the officer should avoid

9.___

A. verbal tracking or requests for clarification
B. open-ended questions
C. sustained eye contact
D. attentive body language

10. Which of the following statements about rape is FALSE?

10.___

A. The use of alcohol and drugs can reduce sexual inhibitions.
B. Rape is a crime of violence.
C. Rape is a crime that can only be committed against women.
D. It is not a sustainable legal charge if the partner has already consented to sex in the past.

11. A person's individual code of ethics is typically determined by each of the following factors, EXCEPT

11.___

A. reason
B. religion
C. emotion
D. law

12. Officer Long, new to the urban precinct where he is assigned patrol, has received a pair   12.____
of complaints from two customers about the owner of a local convenience store, who
works the cash register on most days. According to one customer, the owner became
angry and ordered her out of the store after she had asked the price of a certain item.
The other customer claims that on another occasion, the owner pulled a handgun from
behind the counter and trained it on him as he walked slowly out of the store with his
hands up. Each of the customers has lived in the neighborhood for many years and has
never before seen or heard of any strange behavior on the owner's part.
In investigating these complaints, Officer Long should suspect that

    A. the owner should be considered armed and dangerous, and any entry into the
store should be made with weapons drawn
    B. the cause of the problem is most likely the onset of a serious psychological distur-
bance
    C. the customers may have reasons to be untruthful about the convenience store
owner
    D. the store owner has probably experienced a recent trauma, such as a robbery
attempt or a personal loss

13. Typical signs and symptoms of stress include   13.____
    I. weakened immune system
    II. prolonged, vivid daydreams
    III. insomnia
    IV. depression

    A. I only
    B. I, III and IV
    C. III and IV
    D. I, II, III and IV

14. Other than solid, ethical police work, an officer's best defense against a lawsuit or com-   14.____
plaint is usually

    A. detailed case records
    B. a capable advocate
    C. a vigorous counterclaim against the plaintiff
    D. the testimony of professional character witnesses

15. Assertive people   15.____

    A. avoid stating feelings, opinions, or desires
    B. appear passive, but behave aggressively
    C. state their views and needs directly
    D. appear aggressive, but behave passively

16. In the non-verbal communication process, meaning is most commonly provided by   16.____

    A. body language
    B. touch
    C. tone of voice
    D. context

17. The most obvious practical benefit that deviance has on a society is the   17.___

    A. advancement of the status quo
    B. vindication of new laws
    C. inducement to reach cultural goals
    D. promotion of social unity

18. What is the term for policing that focuses on providing a wider and more thorough array   18.___
of social services to defeat the social problems that cause crime?

    A. Reflective policing
    B. Order maintenance
    C. Social engineering
    D. Holistic policing

19. The term "active listening" mostly refers to a person's ability to   19.___

    A. both listen and accomplish other tasks at the same time
    B. take an active role in determining which information is provided by the speaker
    C. concentrate on what is being said
    D. indicate with numerous physical cues that he/she is listening

20. Police officers in any jurisdiction are most likely to receive calls about   20.___

    A. threats
    B. suspicious persons
    C. petty theft or property crime
    D. disturbances, such as family arguments

21. Which of the following is NOT a physiological explanation for rape?   21.___

    A. uncontrollable sex drive
    B. lack of available partners
    C. reaction to repressed desires
    D. consequence of the natural selection process.

22. Which of the following is an element of self-discipline?   22.___

    A. Establishing and reaching short-term goals
    B. Establishing and reaching long-term goals
    C. Taking an honest look at one's lifestyle and making conscious changes toward improvement
    D. Taking an honest look at one's personality and revealing traits, both good and bad, to others

23. Most of the events in a person's life are the result of   23.___

    A. chance events
    B. a sense of intuition
    C. individual choices and decisions
    D. the decisions of one's parents or other authority figures

24. Which of the following is the most effective way for a department to limit the discretion exercised by police officers?   24._____

    A. Open and flexible departmental directives
    B. Close supervision by departmental management
    C. Broadening role definitions for officers.
    D. Statutory protection from civil liability lawsuits

25. Police officers who demonstrate critical thinking skills are also more likely to demonstrate each of the following, EXCEPT   25._____

    A. the ability to empathize
    B. the tendency to criticize
    C. self-awareness
    D. reflective thinking

KEY (CORRECT ANSWERS)

1.	A	11.	D
2.	B	12.	D
3.	A	13.	B
4.	C	14.	A
5.	C	15.	C
6.	B	16.	A
7.	B	17.	D
8.	B	18.	D
9.	C	19.	C
10.	D	20.	D

21.	C
22.	C
23.	C
24.	B
25.	B

TEST 2

DIRECTIONS: Each question or incomplete statement is followed by several suggested answers or completions. Select the one the BEST answers the question or completes the statement. *PRINT THE LETTER OF THE CORRECT ANSWER IN THE SPACE AT THE RIGHT.*

1. Officer Park responds to a domestic disturbance call to find a mother and her two young children huddled together in the living room, all of them crying. The mother explains that her husband is no longer there; he flew into a fit of rage and then stormed out to join his friends for a night of drinking. Officer Park's first action would most likely be to   1.___

    A. determine the location of the husband
    B. contact the appropriate social services agency, to arrange a consultation
    C. try to calm the family down and ask the mother to explain what happened
    D. refer the mother to a local battered-spouse shelter

2. Most commonly, the reason for crimes involving stranger violence is   2.___

    A. anger
    B. retaliation
    C. hate
    D. robbery

3. For a police officer, "burst stress" is most likely to be caused by   3.___

    A. a shootout
    B. financial troubles
    C. departmental politics
    D. substance abuse

4. The most significant factor in whether a person achieves success in his/her personal life, school, and career is   4.___

    A. intelligence
    B. a positive attitude
    C. existing financial resources
    D. innate ability

5. Typically, a professional code of ethics   5.___

    A. embodies a broad picture of expected moral conduct.
    B. is voluntary
    C. provides specific guidance for performance in situations
    D. are decided by objective ethicists outside of the profession

6. Components recognized by contemporary society as elements of sexual harassment include   6.___
    I. abuse of power
    II. immature behavior
    III. sexual desire
    IV. hormonal imbalance

A. I only
B. I and III
C. II and III
D. I, II, III and IV

7. The phrase "substance abuse" is typically defined as   7.____

    A. an addiction to an illegal substance
    B. the continued use of a psychoactive substance even after it creates problems in a person's life
    C. the overuse of an illegal substance
    D. a situation in which a person craves a drug and organizes his or her life around obtaining it

8. The humanist perspective of behavior holds that people who commit crimes or otherwise   8.____
act badly are

    A. willfully disregarding societal norms
    B. reacting to the deprivation of basic needs
    C. suffering from a psychological illness
    D. experiencing a moral lapse

9. Which of the following is NOT involved in the process of empathic listening?   9.____

    A. actually hearing exactly what the other person is saying
    B. searching for the "hidden meanings" behind statements
    C. listening without judgement
    D. communicating that you're hearing what the other person is saying, both verbally and nonverbally

10. Which of the following is NOT a component in developing a stress-resistant lifestyle?   10.____

    A. Finding leisure time
    B. Eating nutritious foods
    C. Getting enough sleep
    D. Seeking financial independence

11. Which of the following was NOT a factor that led to the expansion of a community polic-   11.____
ing model?

    A. Information obtained at a crime scene during a preliminary investigation was the most important factor determining the probability of an arrest.
    B. Police response times typically had little to do with the probability of making an arrest.
    C. Traditional "preventive patrols" generally failed to reduce crime.
    D. People who knew police officers personally often tried to take advantage of them.

12. Most of the correspondence in a pyramid scheme that has defrauded several elderly vic-   12.____
tims has been traced to a post office box in a rural area. Probably the simplest and most
efficient way of arresting the suspect(s) in this case would be to

    A.   use an elderly man as a "victim" to lure the suspects into an attempt to defraud him
    B.   address a letter to the post office box asking the user to come in for questioning
    C.   check Postal Service records to see who is leasing the post office box
    D.   physically observe the post office box for a while, to see who is using it

13.   The process of hiring a police officer typically involves each of the following, EXCEPT   13.___

    A.   technical preparation
    B.   medical examination
    C.   background checks
    D.   physical ability test

14.   The most common form of rape is _____ rape.   14.___

    A.   stranger
    B.   acquaintance
    C.   sadistic rape
    D.   spousal rape

15.   Officer Stevens and his partner respond to a domestic disturbance call involving a father   15.___
and his teenage daughter. As the officers arrive at their home, the two are still arguing
heatedly, but when the officers enter, the daughter retreats to the kitchen, where she con-
tinues crying. The father explains that his wife, the daughter's mother, died last year, and
the daughter's behavior and school performance have suffered as a result. The father is
afraid that the daughter is falling in with the wrong crowd, and may be getting involved
with drugs. He is afraid for her and doesn't know what to do.
Within the scope of his police role, the most appropriate action for Officer Stevens to
take in this case would be to

    A.   warn both the father and the daughter of the potential consequences of conviction
         on a charge of disturbing the peace
    B.   refer the father and the daughter to a social services or counseling agency
    C.   inform the daughter of the drug statutes that may apply in her case as a way to
         influence her choices
    D.   question the daughter about her feelings surrounding the death of her mother

16.   During an interview, a suspect confesses to the rape of a co-worker that occurred in the   16.___
office after the rest of the employees had left for the day. The suspect says he was tor-
mented by the seductive behavior of the co-worker until he could no longer stand it. He
was himself a victim, he says. In this case, the suspect is making use of the psychological defense mechanism known as

    A.   projection
    B.   regression
    C.   denial
    D.   sublimation

17.   Which of the following is NOT a good stress-reduction strategy?   17.___

    A.   Spend some time each day doing absolutely nothing
    B.   Become more assertive
    C.   Develop a hobby
    D.   Have a sense of humor

18. The term for the policing style which emphasizes problem-solving is _____ style. 18.____

    A. watchman
    B. order maintenance
    C. service
    D. legalistic

19. According to current rules and statutes, any employer 19.____

    A. may inquire as to a job applicant's age or date of birth
    B. may keep on file information regarding an employee's race, color, religion, sex, or national origin.
    C. may refuse employment to someone without a car
    D. must give a woman who has taken time off for maternity leave her same job and salary when she is ready to return to work

20. During a conversation with the mother of a teenage boy who has been arrested twice for shoplifting, an officer attempts to be an active listener as the mother explains why she thinks the boy is having so much trouble. Being an active listener includes each of the following strategies, EXCEPT 20.____

    A. putting the speaker at ease
    B. interrupting with questions to clarify meaning
    C. summarizing the speaker's major ideas and feelings
    D. withholding criticism

21. Which of the following is NOT a characteristic of the typical poverty-class family? 21.____

    A. Female-headed, single-parent families
    B. Unwed parents
    C. Isolated from neighbors and relatives
    D. High divorce rates

22. When speaking with community members about improving the quality of life in the neighborhood, an officer should look for signs of social desirability bias among the people with whom he's talking. Social desirability bias often causes people to 22.____

    A. judge other people based on their social role rather than inner character
    B. attribute their successes to skill, while blaming external factors for failures
    C. modify their interactions or behaviors based on what they think is acceptable to others
    D. contend for leadership positions

23. For a number of reasons, Officer Stone thinks a fellow officer might have a drinking problem, and decides to talk to her about it. The officer says she doesn't have a drinking problem; she doesn't even take a drink until after it gets dark. Her answer indicates that she 23.____

    A. doesn't have a drinking problem
    B. is probably a social drinker
    C. drinks more during the winter months
    D. is in denial

24. Factors which shape the police role include each of the following, EXCEPT 24.__

    A. individual goals
    B. role expectations
    C. role acquisition
    D. multiple-role phenomenon

25. "Deviance" is a social term denoting 25.__

    A. any violation of norms
    B. any serious violation of norms
    C. a type of nonconforming behavior recognizable in all cultures
    D. a specific set of crime statistics

KEY (CORRECT ANSWERS)

1. C		11. D
2. D		12. D
3. A		13. A
4. B		14. B
5. A		15. B
6. A		16. A
7. B		17. A
8. B		18. C
9. B		19. B
10. D		20. B

21. C
22. C
23. D
24. A
25. A

EXAMINATION SECTION
TEST 1

DIRECTIONS: Each question or incomplete statement is followed by several suggested answers or completions. Select the one that BEST answers the question or completes the statement. *PRINT THE LETTER OF THE CORRECT ANSWER IN THE SPACE AT THE RIGHT.*

Questions 1-3.

DIRECTIONS: Questions 1 to 3 measure your ability to fill out forms correctly and to remember information and ideas. Below and on the following two pages are directions for completing two kinds of forms, a correctly completed sample of each form, and a section from a procedures manual. You should memorize the sets of directions and the section from the procedures manual.

In the test, you will be (1) asked questions about the information and ideas in the manual and (2) presented with completed forms and asked to identify entries that are INCORRECT (contain wrong information, incomplete information, information in wrong order, etc.).

DIRECTIONS FOR COMPLETING CASE REPORT FORM

A case report form (see completed sample) is to be filled out by each officer at the time of the preliminary investigation. The entry for each numbered box is as follows:

Box 1 - The time the assignment was received.

Box 2 - The day, date, and time of the occurrence, in that order. Names of months and days may be abbreviated.

Box 3 - The manner in which the report was received. Use P = person, TOC = Through Official Channels (911 or other emergency numbers), M = mail, or T = telephone.

Box 4 - Name of the person notifying the department.

Box 5 - The address of the occurrence. include number, street, and village, and name of establishment, if appropriate. Do NOT abbreviate the name of a street, village, or establishment. If no street address is available, supply directions.

Box 6 - Victim's name, last name first.

Box 7 - Victim's birthdate - month, day, and year. Use the style shown in the completed sample.

Box 8 - Victim's sex and race: F = female, M = male, B = black, W = white, Y = yellow, O = other.

Box 9 - Relationship of victim to the offender (be as specific as possible):
HU = husband, WI = wife, MO = mother, FA = father,

SO = son, DA = daughter, BR = brother, SI = sister,
AQ = acquaintance, ST = stranger, UN = unknown.

SAMPLE OF COMPLETED CASE REPORT FORM

1. Time Received 5:57 PM		2. Date and Time of Occurrence Wed., Oct. 17, 2007, 1:00 PM	
3. Original Complaint Received TOC		4. Reported by Jeffrey Greene	
5. Place of Occurrence Sam's Stationery Shop, 130 Main St., Brooketown			
6. Victim's Name Silver, Sam	7. Date of Birth 3/17/62		8. Sex and Race M - W
7. Relationship to the Offender ST			

DIRECTIONS FOR COMPLETING
AUTOMOBILE FIELD INTERVIEW FORM

An automobile field interview form (see completed sample on the following page) is to be filled out when a car is stopped under suspicious circumstances, but no arrests are made. The entry for each numbered box is as follows:

Box 1 - Driver's name, last name first.

Box 2 - Village of residence, if within the county

Box 3 - Type of vehicle: S = sedan, C = convertible, SW = station wagon, V = van, T = truck.

Box 4 - Vehicle registration number.

Box 5 - Time and place of interview: location (street address only), time (per 24-hour clock), date, in that order.

Box 6 - Type of area: C = commercial, H = highway, R = residential, I = industrial, S = school

Box 7 - Patrol post number: precinct number is first digit; sector number is last two digits.

Box 8 - Officer's name and shield number, in that order.

SAMPLE OF COMPLETED AUTOMOBILE FIELD INTERVIEW FORM

1. Operator Robbins, Susan		2. Village Shady Brook	
3. Type of Vehicle C		4. Registration C 7237	
5. Time and Place of Interview Merry Road at Elm Street, 1428, 2/7/07			
6. Type of Area R	7. Post No. 221		8. Officer Sally Dodd, 2212

CASE REPORT MANUAL
Section 1 - Solvability Factors

A solvability factor can be defined as any information about a crime that can provide a means to determine who committed it. In other words, a solvability factor is a useful clue to the identity of the perpetrator.

Based on national-level research, the following twelve universal factors have been identified:

1. Existence of witnesses to the crime
2. Knowledge of a perpetrator's name
3. Knowledge of a perpetrator's whereabouts
4. Description of a perpetrator
5. Identification of a perpetrator
6. Property that has traceable characteristics such as a registration number
7. Existence of a distinctive MO
8. Presence of significant physical evidence such as a set of burglar's tools
9. Description of a perpetrator's automobile
10. Positive results from a crime scene evidence search, such as fingerprints or footprints
11. Belief that a crime may be solved with publicity and/or reasonable investigative effort
12. Opportunity for only one person to have committed the crime

The presence of at least one of these solvability factors is necessary for there to be a reasonable chance for a solution to the crime. When there is no solvability factor, the chance of crime solution is limited. Therefore, the police officer who arrives at the scene of a crime first must make the greatest possible effort to identify solvability factors. This effort should include identification of witnesses and a thorough search of the crime scene.

DIRECTIONS: After you have memorized the directions and manual section, try to answer the following questions without referring to the study materials.

1. Which of the following crimes is *most likely* to have a solvability factor?   1.____

   A. A pickpocket takes several wallets on a crowded bus.
   B. Two muggers take money from a blind man in an alley.
   C. A hospital drug cabinet is broken into during a major emergency.
   D. A kidnapper escapes in a van decorated with pink, yellow, and avocado-green paint.

2. At 7:30 AM on Wednesday, February 6, 2007, Patrol Officer Alex White was assigned to   2.____
   investigate a suspected child-beating. The boy had been brought to the hospital, and Dr. Paul Cohen called the local station house at 7:20 AM. David Pepson, a White boy born on June 27, 2005, was brought from his home by his mother, who claims that her husband had punished David an hour earlier for making loud noises. David resides with his parents at 86 Whitewood Lane in Middletown.

CASE REPORT FORM

1. Time Received 7:30 AM		2. Date and Time of Occurrence Wed., February 6, 2007, 5:00 AM	
3. Original Complaint Received T		4. Reported by Dr. Paul Cohen	
5. Place of Occurrence 86 Whitewood Lane, Middletown			
6. Victim's Name David Pepson	7. Date of Birth 6/27/05		8. Sex and Race M - W
9. Relationship to the Offender FA			

Of the following, the box in the form above which is filled out INCORRECTLY is Box
   A. 3   B. 4   C. 8   D. 9

3. Officer Steven Brown, 7234, stopped a station wagon in the business section of Westville. He talked to the driver, John Caseman, on Rocky Road near South Bend and the western boundary of section 16 of precinct 2 at 8:20 PM on 3/8/87. The vehicle, registration number 2729H belongs to Mr. Caseman, who resides in Silverton.

AUTOMOBILE FIELD INTERVIEW FORM

1. Operator Caseman, John		2. Village Westville	
3. Type of Vehicle V		4. Registration 2729H	
5. Time and Place of Interview Rocky Road near South Bend, 2020, 3/8/07			
6. Type of Area C	7. Post No. 216		8. Officer Steven Brown, 7234

Of the following, the box in the form above which is filled out INCORRECTLY is Box
   A. 1   B. 3   C. 5   D. 7

Questions 4-6.

DIRECTIONS: Questions 4 to 6 measure your ability to recall information in a set of bulletins. To do well in the test, you must memorize both the pictorial and the written portions of each of the following eight bulletins.

Date of Issuance 5/13/07

INFORMATION
WANTED

by

Police Department. County of Allamin
Hooblertown, Indiana 43102

The Allamin County Police Department homicide squad requests all auto repair shops, dealers and General Motors parts dealers in the precinct be contacted and questioned relative to the below described vehicle which is wanted for a felony - leaving the scene of a fatality. If vehicle is located, contact the homicide squad, (731) 624-1372. Refer to Homicide Case 130.

Place of Occurrence:	Midway State Road, South Strata, Indiana
Time of Occurrence:	0240 hours on March 3, 2007
Vehicle Wanted:	1980 Oldsmobile Cutlass Supreme, color green
Damage:	The Vehicle will have damage to the plastic grill located in the vicinity of the right front headlights. The chrome strip which is affixed to the center of the hood was recovered at the scene.
Parts:	The following parts will be needed to repair the vehicle: 1. Hood - GM Part No. 557547 or 557557 2. Plastic Grill - GM Part No. 22503156

<u>W A N T E D</u>
<u>by</u>

BULLETIN NO.
9-05

<u>Police Department. County of Paradise</u>
<u>Cobbs Cove, Louisiana 41723</u>
<u>for</u>
<u>MURDER</u>

No. FJ110M

Note
Seiko watch with Gold Face and three section band is not a standard import into this area.

Occurrence:	Blue Jay Way and Nickel Drive, Yellowbird, 0530 hours on April 12, 2005.
Modus Operandi:	The deceased returned to his home at 2 Blue Jay Way, Yellowbird, at about 0530 hours, April 12, 2005. Four male whites were waiting in the vicinity of his garage and robbed him of U.S. currency and the above watch. They ran to the intersection of Blue Jay Way and Nickel Drive and got into a late model, shiny dark color, four door sedan with large tail-lights. The deceased chased them to the corner. One shot was fired causing his death.
Subjects:	Four Male Whites, dark hair.
Property:	One Seiko Quartz - Sports 100 - wrist watch, yellow metal face and crystal retainer. The band is an expandable three-section, white, yellow, white metal.
Note:	Anyone with information is requested to contact the Paradise County Homicide Squad.

W A N T E D
by
Police Department. County of Whitewall
Short Hills, Kentucky 27135

BULLETIN NO.
15- 05

for
MURDER

RC-550JW/C

Occurrence:	Public street, Brown Avenue, 60 ft. north of Camino Street, South Hill, KY, at 2340 hours, 6/25/05.
Modus Operandi:	The victim of the murder was walking south on Brown Avenue when he was accosted by the suspect and shot in the head by the suspect.
Subject:	Male, Black, 25-28 years, 5'9"-6' tall, thin build, short dark hair, medium dark skin, wearing a dark waist-length jacket, sneakers - armed with a gun.
Property:	The above property, a JVC AM-FM cassette radio, Model RC 550JW/C made of black plastic with chrome trim was stolen during the commission of a murder on Brown Avenue in South Hill. The battery compartment door is missing from the radio.
Note:	Anyone with information concerning the murder or the radio is asked to call the Whitewall Homicide Squad.

<u>W A N T E D</u>
<u>by</u>
<u>Police Department, County of Larinda</u>
<u>Blue Ridge. CA 97235</u>

<u>for</u>
<u>BURGLARY</u>

BULLETIN NO.
6-05

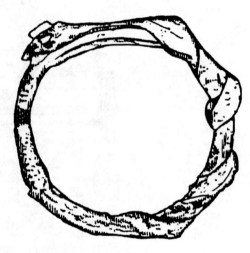

#1

#2

Date of Occurrence: August 17, 2005 - 1930 to 2230 hours.
Place of Occurrence: Private home, 37 Cliffmount Dr., Palasino, CA
Property: Two distinctive, original designer rings taken.
    1. Ladies, yellow gold, 18K ring, size 8, an alligator with green emerald eye.
    2. Mans, yellow gold ring, a snake with 1/4 carat white diamond head and white diamond chips for eyes .
Value: 1. $5,000   2. $7,500
Note: Any information - contact Burglary Squad, Refer to DD 4-25.

WANTED
by

BULLETIN NO.
12-05

Police Department, County of Canton
Midship. Texas 84290

for
BURGLARY

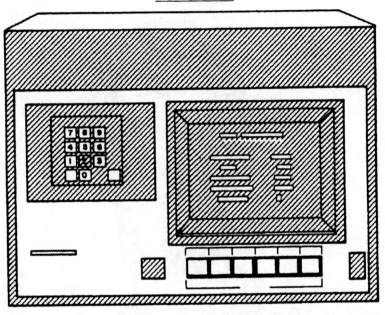

Date of Occurrence:	July 31, 2005 - 1640 hours to August 1 - 0720 hours.
Place of Occurrence:	606 Hillmont Drive, Alston, TX Freemont Testing Systems
Property:	Three engine analysers, color red, measuring 14" x 20" x 19"
Serial Numbers:	1. AN-0059 2. BP-0079 3. CR-0099
Value:	$6,666.00 each.
Note:	Request officers on patrol check service stations on post for the above items. Any information contact Detective Bryant, Third Squad, and refer to DD 3-52.

<u>W A N T E D</u>
<u>by</u>

<u>Police Department, County of Marina</u>
<u>Waterford, CT 03612</u>

<u>for</u>
<u>ROBBERY</u>

2004 PHOTO

Occurrences:	Robberies of gas stations and boutiques in North End precincts of Marina County.
Modus Operandi:	Subject enters store and uses telephone or shops. He then produces sawed-off shotgun or revolver from under his coat and announces robbery.
Subject:	Harry Hamilton, Male, White, DOB 6/22/63, 5'10", 180 lbs., medium complexion, severely pockmarked face.
Further Details:	Contact Robbery Squad at (203) 832-7663. Refer to Robbery Case 782. Robbery Squad has warrant for subject. IF THIS PERSON ENTERS YOUR STORE <u>DIAL 911</u> OR THE ABOVE NUMBER

W A N T E D
by

BULLETIN NO.
30-04

Police Department, County of Panfield
Lanser, South Carolina 30012

for
ROBBERY

2004 PHOTO
#2

#1

Occurrence:	3 North Avenue, Anita, South Carolina, on 11/26/04 at 2310 hours.
Modus Operandi:	The above subjects forced their way into the private residence of a rug dealer, accosted the dealer, his wife, and brother, demanding jewelry, currency, escaped on foot after binding victims.
Subjects:	No. 1 - Male, White, 40-45 years, 200 lbs., heavy build, bald shaved head, fair complexion, mustache, goatee, large hooked nose, black leather jacket, armed with a knife. No. 2 - Male, White, 6'1" tall, medium build, brown hair, subject identified as Mark Nine, DOB 4/16/68, last known address 1275 East 61st Street, Brooklyn, NY in 2001, hard drug user, armed with a hand gun, subject has been indicted for residence robbery. See Wanted Bulletin 21-02.
Possible 3rd Suspect:	Male, Hispanic, 30-35 years, 5'6", thin build, collar-length black wavy hair, eyes close together, with a large Doberman. Subject observed in the area before robbery talking to bald, stocky male. Also seen entering a vehicle containing 3 or 4 males after the robbery.
Loss:	U.S. currency and jewelry valued at $3,000 to $4,000.

Further Details: Contact Robbery Squad.

WANTED
by
Police Department, County of Fantail
Sweet Waters, Vermont 04610

BULLETIN NO.
1-05

for
HI-JACKING

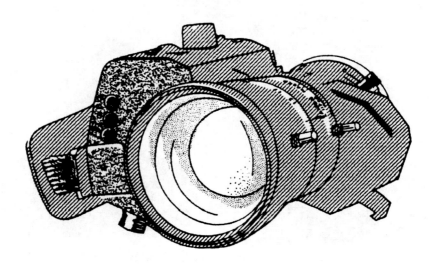

Occurrence:	Vicinity of Nikon Plaza, off Jewel Avenue & Brook Bubble Road, Sweet Waters, VT at 1820 hours, 2/6/05.
Modus Operandi:	Subjects accosted the driver of a United Parcel tractor/trailer, forcing him into a pale yellow van-type vehicle, make and year unknown. Vehicle contained a black and yellow leopard rug. Driver released after two (2) hours, in the vicinity of West Lake, VT. Tractor/ trailer recovered in White River, New Hampshire.
Subjects:	Four (4) male Whites, one possibly named Joe, armed with hand guns. No further description.
Loss:	Photo of above item: one (1) of four (4) broadcasting TV zoom lenses made by Nikon, valued at $7,000. Also included in the Nikon loss were current models of cameras, lenses, calculators, valued at $196,000. Medical supplies, mfg. by True Tell Inc., value $49,000. High quality medical examination scopes, industrial fiberscopes, cassette recorders and cameras, all mgf. by Canon Inc. valued at over $250,000. Sweaters, young mens, vee-neck design, mfg. Milford, Inc., labeled Dimension, Robt. Klein, J.C. Penney. Valued at over $20,450. Above items bearing serial numbers have been entered in NCIC.

Further Details: Contact Robbery Squad.

DIRECTIONS: After you have memorized both the pictorial and written portions of the bulletins, try to answer the following questions WITHOUT referring to the study materials.

4. Which of the following statements about the contents of the *Information Wanted* bulletin 4._____
is or are true?

      I.   The subject vehicle is involved in a felony.

      II.   The subject vehicle is green-colored.

The CORRECT answer is:

  A. I *only*   B. II *only*

  C. Both I and II   D. Neither I nor II

5. 5._____

Which of the following statements about the object above is or are true?

      I.   It was taken in the robbery of a residence.

      II.   Its value is between $1,000 and $2,000.

The CORRECT answer is:

  A. I *only*   B. II *only*

  C. Both I and II   D. Neither I nor II

6. Which of the following, if any, fits the description of the individual who is wanted for the 6._____
robbery of several gas stations?

  A.   B.

C.

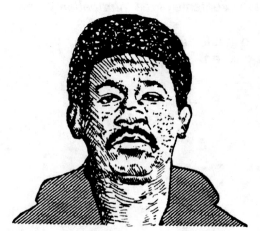

D.   None of these

Questions 7-10.

DIRECTIONS: Questions 7 to 10 measure your ability to memorize and recall addresses, identification numbers and codes, and similar data.
In the test, you will be asked questions about the following body of information. You will NOT have the information in front of you when you take the test.

RADIO SIGNALS
01 - Back in Service
02 - Acknowledgement(OK)
06 - On Coffee
08 - Off Meal, Coffee, Personal
27 - Valid License
33 - Clear Channel (Any Emergency Request)
41 - One-Car Assistance Request
63 - Responding to Command
78 - Police Officer in Danger
99 - Possible Emergency Situation, Respond Quietly

TRUCK-TRACTOR IDENTIFICATION NUMBERS
VIN* Plate

Make	Location
Autocar......................	8
Brockway...................	2
Diamond Reo...........	9
Ford...........................	10
GMC........................	4
Kenworth...................	1
Peterbuilt..................	7
White.........................	5

*Vehicle
 Identification
 Number

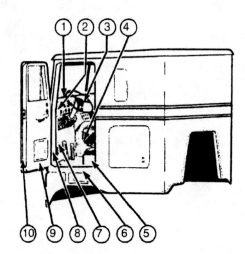

Location of County Precinct Houses

First -   In H,* on S side of Merrick Rd., just E of Grand Avenue.
Second -   In OB,* 1/8 mi. E of Seaford-Oyster Bay Expressway, 1/8 mi.S. of Jericho Trnpk.
Third -   In NH,* 1/8 mi. N of Hillside Ave., 1/8 mi. W of Willis Avenue
Fourth -   In H, on E side of Broadway, just N of Rockaway Avenue
Fifth -   In H, on S side of Dutch Broadway, 1/4 mi. N of Exit 14 of Southern State Parkway
Six -   In NH, just E of Community Drive, and just S of Whitney Pond Park. Seventh - In H,
                 on side of Merrick Rd., just W of Seaford-Oyster Bay Expressway
Eighth -   In H, on E side of Wantagh Ave., just N of Hempstead Farmingdale Trnpk.

Location of Universities, Colleges, and Institutes

Adelphi U. -   In H,* 1/4 mi. E of Nassau Blvd., 1/4 mi. S of Stewart Ave.
Hofstra U. -   In H, at Oak and Fulton Streets.
Molloy College -   In H, on Hempstead Ave., just S of Southern State Pkway., and midway
                              between Exits 19 and 20.
C. W. Post College - In OB,* on Northern Blvd., 1 1/2 mi. W of Massapequa-Glen Cove Rd.
Nassau Community College - In H, on Stewart Ave., 1/2 mi. E of Clinton Rd.
Long Island Agri. & Tech. Institute - In OB, 1/2 mi. E of Round Swamp Rd., between Bethpage
          State Park and Old Bethpage Village Restoration.
N.Y. Inst. of Technology - In OB, on Northern Blvd., just E of line dividing OB and NH.
U.S. Merchant Marine Acad. - In NH,* at NW end of Elm Point Rd.

---

*H - Town of Hempstead; NH - Town of North Hempstead; OB - Town of Oyster Bay.

DIRECTIONS: After you have memorized the listed data, try to answer the following questions
                     WITHOUT referring to the list.

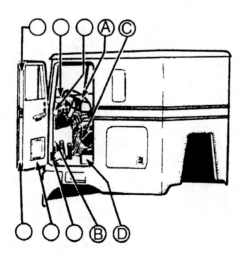

7.   On a GMC truck-tractor, above, the VIN is located at   7.____

         A. A   B. B   C. C   D. D

8.   The radio signal for *back in service* is   8.____

         A. 01   B. 04   C. 08   D.   none of these

9. The Third Precinct House is located in   9.__

    A. NH, 1/8 mi. N of Hillside Ave., 1/8 mi. W of Willis Ave.
    B. NH, 1/4 mi. S of I.U. Willets Rd., 1/4 mi. E of Herricks Rd.
    C. Williston Park, on Willis Ave., 1/4 mi. S of Northern State Parkway
    D. Mineola, on Mineola Blvd., 1/2 mi. N of Jericho Trnpk.

10. The U.S. Merchant Marine Academy is at the NW end of _____ Rd.   10.__

    A. Sands Point   B. Mill Neck
    C. Kings Point   D. Elm Point

KEY (CORRECT ANSWERS)

1.	D	6.	D
2.	D	7.	C
3.	B	8.	A
4.	C	9.	A
5.	A	10.	D

———

VISUAL RECALL
EXAMINATION SECTION

PICTURE BOOKLET

DIRECTIONS: You will have five minutes to memorize as much as possible of all the details in the pictures. The pictures include a street scene and various faces. You may not write or make any notes while studying the pictures. The test will be based on these pictures.

After five minutes, close the Picture Booklet and do not look at the pictures again. Then, answer the questions that follow.

Street Scene

While on foot-patrol, you receive a call on your portable police radio that a robbery may be in progress at a watch repair shop. It so happens that the shop is across the street from where you are standing. What you see at this moment will help you decide what to do, and remembering what you see may be very important later on.

Study this scene carefully. You will be asked questions about it in this examination.

Faces

Below are twelve photographs taken from FBI files. Study the twelve faces carefully. Your ability to remember these faces will be tested in this examination.

RECALL OF DETAILS

DIRECTIONS: Questions 1 through 5 test your ability to remember the details of the street scene at the beginning of this examination. Each question is followed by four choices. Choose the one BEST answer (A, B, C, or D). *PRINT THE LETTER OF THE CORRECT ANSWER IN THE SPACE AT THE RIGHT.*

1. The boy by the dark-colored car
   A. had on dark glasses
   B. was a lookout
   C. had on a jacket
   D. wore an 'Afro' haircut

   1._____

2. The group of men on the sidewalk were
   A. facing one another
   B. looking at the watch repair shop
   C. all African-American
   D. talking and laughing

   2._____

3. Nearest to the watch repair shop was a
   A. boy standing by a dark-colored car
   B. woman in a doorway
   C. group of men on the sidewalk
   D. man next to a light-colored car

   3._____

4. The dark-colored car
   A. was a four-door sedan
   B. carried New York State plates
   C. was headed uptown
   D. had a man in the driver's seat

   4._____

5. A woman on the sidewalk appeared to be
   A. looking at the apartment windows directly above her
   B. looking toward the watch repair shop
   C. watching the boy by the dark-colored car
   D. coming out of a store

   5._____

RECOGNITION OF FACES

DIRECTIONS: Questions 6 through 15 test your ability to recognize faces that you have seen before. Each test number is followed by three faces. If one of the three faces was among the FBI photographs that you studied at the beginning of the examination, select its letter (A, B or C). If *none* of the three faces was among the FBI photographs, select the letter D. (Do not forget that every question has a fourth choice.) *PRINT THE LETTER OF THE CORRECT ANSWER IN THE SPACE AT THE RIGHT.*

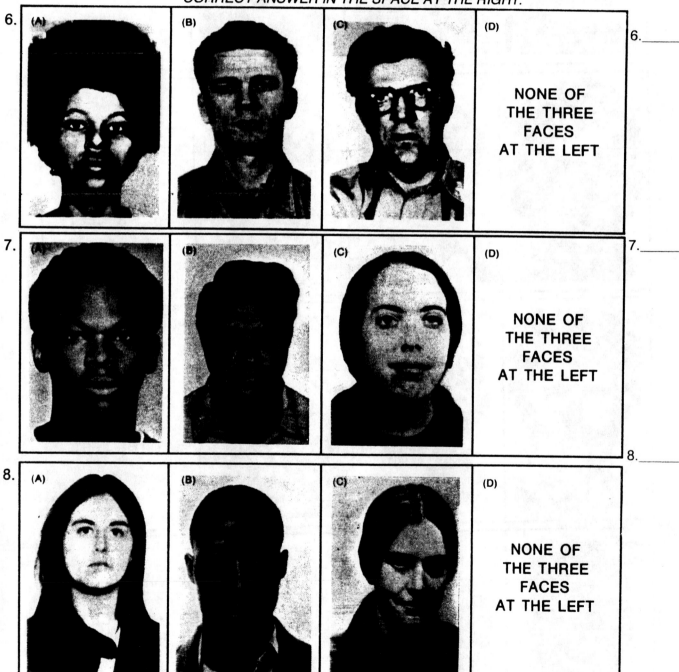

6. (A) (B) (C) (D) NONE OF THE THREE FACES AT THE LEFT

6._____

7. (A) (B) (C) (D) NONE OF THE THREE FACES AT THE LEFT

7._____

8._____

8. (A) (B) (C) (D) NONE OF THE THREE FACES AT THE LEFT

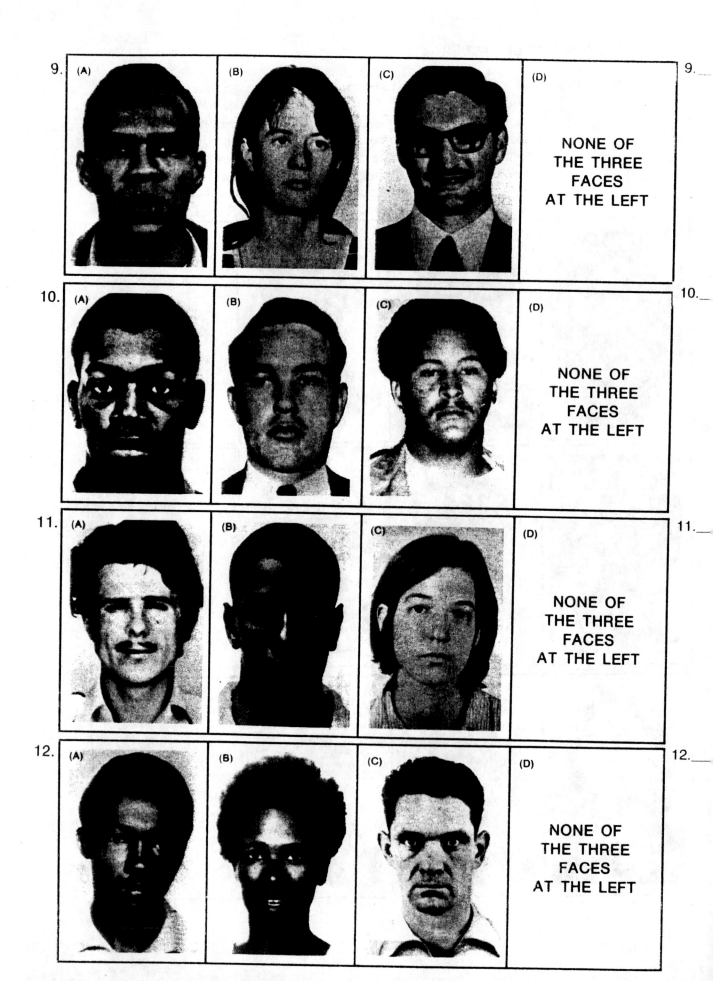

9. (A) (B) (C) (D) NONE OF THE THREE FACES AT THE LEFT

10. (A) (B) (C) (D) NONE OF THE THREE FACES AT THE LEFT

11. (A) (B) (C) (D) NONE OF THE THREE FACES AT THE LEFT

12. (A) (B) (C) (D) NONE OF THE THREE FACES AT THE LEFT

KEY (CORRECT ANSWERS)

1. C	6. B	11. B
2. A	7. D	12. B
3. D	8. D	13. A
4. A	9. B	14. C
5. B	10. C	15. B

PROBLEM SENSITIVITY

This section of the exam measures your ability to choose the course of action that should be taken <u>first</u> in critical situations.

<u>Sample Questions</u>

1. What should an officer do <u>first</u> when investigating an incident?   1.____

   A. Write a report of the incident.
   B. Inform other police officers of the incident.
   C. Proceed to the scene of the incident.
   D. Interview witnesses.

Getting the correct information to the emergency medical personnel is extremely important. It is suggested that you, the police officer, make the call if possible, or assign the task to a person who appears calm. If you are alone at the accident scene, do not leave the victim until breathing is restored, all bleeding has been stopped, the victim is no longer in danger of further injury, and all precautions have been taken against shock. When the emergency medical personnel arrive, brief them as to what happened to the victim, the type of first aid you have administered, and the physical status of the victim.

2. When the emergency medical personnel arrives at the accident scene, you <u>first</u> should   2.____
   tell them:

   A. how long the victim's breathing has been restored.
   B. how long the bleeding has been stopped.
   C. that the victim appeared to be going into shock.
   D. the type of first aid you administered.

———

KEY (CORRECT ANSWERS)

1. C
2. D

———

POLICE PROCEDURES & INFORMATION

Police Officers must be able to understand information and follow specified police procedures. One portion of the exam will test your ability to remember the information presented in this booklet. You are to assume that the police procedures presented here are the procedures that must be followed. The procedures and information to be memorized are:

Hospital Cases
Use of Police Radio
Responsibilities of Police Officers at Crime Scenes
Transporting Prisoners
Reporting Vehicular Accidents
Job Specification for Police Officer Trainee

Carefully learn these police procedures. If there are any words in these procedures you do not understand, look them up in a dictionary. You will NOT have these materials in front of you when you take the test. It is important to learn carefully this information or you will not be able to answer the questions on this section of the test.

Hospital Cases

Police personnel may be assigned to or encounter a hospital case. These cases will be considered emergencies unless a doctor or other medically trained person states otherwise. Hospital cases will be transported to the nearest hospital. In the case of a patient needing specialized care not available at the nearest hospital, a patrol supervisor will be contacted and will make the final decision.

Whenever possible, such as in cases where a stretcher is not needed, hospital cases will be transported by patrol car instead of by patrol wagon. In the case of life-threatening situations, the City Paramedic Unit will be notified immediately. The paramedics will assume the care and transportation of the patient. Police officers will direct traffic and assist paramedics as required.

Use of Police Radio

The purpose of police radio is to receive calls from the general public and dispatch unit, and to aid and inform police personnel in the field. Police dispatchers can give out assignments, relay information, and dispatch supervisors when requested or needed by field officers. Dispatchers cannot make command decisions but can relay the information to the proper command personnel. Police dispatchers also will broadcast information of general interest to police such as names of wanted and missing persons, and information on crimes. In addition, they will assign an identification number to each incident for which an officer is to file a report. This number will be recorded in the proper block on the Incident Report (82-7) and on all subsequent reports resulting from the original incident.

Dispatchers will make assignments by broadcasting the vehicle number, location of assignment and reason (e.g., "214, 2200 Connecticut Avenue, possible child abuse"). Each assignment will be repeated at least three times. If a unit is in-service and does not acknowledge an assignment, the dispatcher will record this and the officer will be required to submit a written memo stating the reason he/she did not respond. Disciplinary action may result.

Units will respond to dispatchers by stating their vehicle number and "Okay" if they can respond to the call. If not, they will state their vehicle number and the reason they are not available. Then the dispatcher may assign another officer. Patrol officers will notify police radio upon arrival at the scene by stating the vehicle number and "on scene." Officers will again notify police radio at the completion of the assignment by stating the vehicle number and "available."

All uniformed officers will remain in radio range at all times unless they are out-of-service or there is a shortage of hand-held units. Officers who will be out of radio range will report to the dispatcher their vehicle number, location, and reason for being out of range (e.g., "214, 2414 Down Drive, no portable unit") and will report back in as soon as they have radio access.

When an officer wishes to contact the dispatcher in a non-emergency situation, he/she will wait for a break in communications and state the vehicle number. The officer will wait for dispatcher acknowledgement (i.e., "214 go ahead") before proceeding. The officer will acknowledge information and assignments by stating vehicle number and "Okay."

In emergency situations, the officer will state his/her vehicle number and "emergency." These calls take precedence and all other transmissions will stop until the emergency call is ended. Emergency calls include: assist officer calls, reports of crimes-in-progress, car accidents involving serious injury, riotous situations, and life-endangering situations.

Responsibilities of Police Officers at Crime Scenes

The first officer on the scene is responsible for protecting the scene and telling the police dispatcher to send the necessary assistance. The officer also will take responsibility for the following:

1. Give first aid to the injured and make arrangements for transportation of the injured immediately. The officer should try to outline the position of the body before removal.

2. Question victim(s), if possible, to find out what happened. Notify police radio so information can be broadcast.

3. Detain all persons at the scene and try to prevent conversations among witnesses.

4. Do not let <u>anyone</u> touch or move anything at the scene or enter the crime scene except:

   A. Those transporting the injured.
   B. Personnel from the investigative unit and crime lab unit. I.D. <u>must</u> be displayed on outer garment.
   C. Police officers guarding the scene.
   D. An object such as a motor vehicle at the scene may be moved if it is a danger to public safety. Before moving it, outline its position and why and when moved. Give this information to the chief investigator on the scene.

5. Maintain a log of the names and badge numbers of all persons entering the scene and the reason for entering.

6. <u>No</u> other personnel, including supervisors not involved in the investigation, are allowed on the crime scene.

Transporting Prisoners

All persons will be searched by the arresting officer in accordance with procedures in section 11.07 of the Patrol Officer's Manual.

All prisoners will be taken to the district station by patrol wagon. If no wagons are available, prisoners will be transported in a patrol car after the officers receive permission from their sergeant. Two officers must be present in the car. The prisoner will sit in the rear seat behind the passenger side and the second officer will sit behind the driver.

All prisoners will be handcuffed behind their backs.

Prisoners should be kept in the rear seat of the patrol car while waiting for the wagon. Officers riding in the wagon will search the prisoner again in accordance with section 11.07 of the Patrol Officer's Manual.

After prisoners have been handed over to other authorities, officers will check their vehicles for contraband or weapons left behind or hidden by the prisoner. Officers should check behind and under seats. In patrol wagons, officers also should check the canvas stretchers and blankets if so equipped. Officers should exercise caution in case razor blades or other dangerous and exposed materials have been left behind.

Reporting Vehicular Accidents

The following procedures will be followed by police officers responding to or observing a vehicular accident:

1. Check to see if there are any injured people who require hospital treatment. If so, use police radio to request transportation.

2. Obtain operator's license(s), registration card(s), and insurance card(s) from the operator(s).

3. Fill out Incident Report for all accidents.

4. If the accident is reportable, also fill out a Police Accident Report. Reportable accidents are those in which any of the following occur:

    A. There is death or injury.
    B. Any vehicle is so damaged that it cannot be driven from the scene of the accident without further damage or danger, and towing is required.
    C. There is any damage to state or local government property or vehicles.
    D. The operator involved leaves the scene of the accident.
    E. It is believed that the operator involved is under the influence of drugs or alcohol.

5. Give operator(s) involved the report number of the completed Police Accident Form.

6. Give each operator an officer's business card containing the officer's rank, name, district of assignment, badge number, and district phone number.

7. Request police radio to send an officer from the Accident Investigation Unit in all cases where there has been fatal or potentially fatal injuries, or a local or state government vehicle is involved.

Note: The job specifications are not official with respect to the position for which you are applying. They are included to test your ability to read, understand, and recall information.

Job Specification for Police Officer Trainee

Nature of Work:

This work applies to entry and training level positions in law enforcement. The officer is trained in all aspects of law enforcement. Often, considerable public contact is involved, therefore, the officer is required to exercise the immediate practical judgment necessary to cope with unusual or emergency situations. The officer is expected to place emphasis on courteous explanation and personal persuasiveness in routinely seeking the compliance of others in obeying the laws. However, situations arise in which the officer must restrain and/or arrest persons threatening the security of the public.

Performance of the work is guided by written procedures. The officer receives close supervision from a higher level police officer. Officers in the trainee class normally do not hold supervisory positions.

Examples of Work:

Patrols assigned areas.
Searches for missing persons.
Compiles data, keeps records, and prepares written reports on enforcement activities.
Enforces federal, state, and local laws.
Issues warnings or summonses and arrests those apprehended for violations.
Investigates accidents and criminal acts.
Presents evidence and gives testimony in court.
Renders emergency first aid.
Gives motorists directions and assistance.
Attends formal training courses.

Required Knowledge and Abilities:

Introductory knowledge of criminal, civil, and traffic laws; and, knowledge of the care and use of firearms.

Ability to handle firearms safely, to comprehend oral and written instructions; to write narrative reports; to meet situations requiring tact, understanding, and good judgment; to detect situations imperiling security and safety; to remember names and faces; to learn.

Minimum Qualifications:

Education: Graduation from high school or possession of a State high school equivalence certificate.

License: A valid Motor Vehicle Operator license.

Conditions of Employment:

1. Candidates will be given a medical examination to determine physical ability to perform the job. This examination may include strength and agility tests. Good vision is required.

2. Due to provisions in the Retirement System Law, candidates aged 70 or over will not be appointed.

3. Duties necessitate being outdoors in all types of weather, standing and walking, or in assigned vehicles.

4. Due to the nature and condition of the work, a criminal conviction record may be a bar to employment. Candidates who have a conviction record will not be prevented from taking the test. If an investigation determines that a criminal conviction record is job-related, the candidate will not be selected and the Department of Personnel will authorize the passing over of such names on the eligible lists as provided by State law.

5. Persons appointed to the position of police officer may be required to be present for duty on Saturdays, Sundays, and holidays. Officers in this position may be assigned to any one of three shifts on a permanent or rotating basis and are required to report to work when called in during emergencies.

6. Demonstration of practical knowledge and proficiency in the safe use and care of fire-arms may be required of applicants prior to appointment or upon completion of the Police Training Commission course.

7. Prior to appointment being made permanent, a person appointed to a position of police officer trainee must have successfully completed, within the first year of employment, a training course approved by the Police Training Commission. Candidates must, therefore, be able to meet the minimum standards as determined by the Police Training Commission.

8. Candidates receiving a passing rating on all parts of the test will be interviewed before appointment. Also, candidates are subject to investigation by the State Police in order to establish eligibility to be commissioned to make arrests and to obtain a gun permit.

9. Persons appointed to this position may be required to have a telephone in their residence so that they may be contacted at any time.

Sample Questions

The following question is based on "Responsibilities of Police Officers at Crime Scenes."

1. You are the first officer on the scene. Your sergeant, who is not part of the investigation, wants to enter the crime scene. You should:

    A.   let him enter.
    B.   let him enter but caution him not to move or touch anything.
    C.   let him enter and record his name and badge number in the log.
    D.   not let him enter.

The following question is based on "Reporting Vehicular Accidents."

2. You arrive at the scene of an accident at the intersection of Apple Street and Orange Avenue. The owner of a badly damaged car tells you she saw a man in a van run into her parked car. You should:

    A. use police radio to broadcast the description of the van.
    B. fill out an Incident Report and a Police Accident Report.
    C. put a tag on the car with the name of the owner and the date of the accident.
    D. question witnesses to verify the car owner's account of the accident.

———

KEY (CORRECT ANSWERS)

1. D

2. B

———

EXAMINATION SECTION
TEST 1

DIRECTIONS: Each question or incomplete statement is followed by several suggested answers or completions. Select the one that BEST answers the question or completes the statement. *PRINT THE LETTER OF THE CORRECT ANSWER IN THE SPACE AT THE RIGHT.*

Questions 1-4.

DIRECTIONS: Questions 1 to 4 measure your ability (1) to determine whether statements from witnesses say essentially the same thing and (2) to determine the evidence needed to make it reasonably certain that a particular conclusion is true.

To do well in this part of the test, you do NOT have to have a working knowledge of police procedures and techniques or to have any more familiarity with crimes and criminal behavior than that acquired from reading newspapers, listening to radio, or watching TV. To do well in this part, you must read carefully and reason closely. Sloppy reading or sloppy reasoning will lead to a low score.

1. In which of the following do the two statements made say essentially the same thing in two different ways?   1.____
    I.   All members of the pro-x group are free from persecution. No person that is persecuted is a member of the pro-x group.
    II. Some responsible employees of the police department are not supervisors. Some police department supervisors are not responsible employees.
    The CORRECT answer is:

    A. I *only*   B. II *only*
    C. Both I and II   D. Neither I nor II

2. In which of the following do the two statements made say essentially the same thing in two different ways?   2.____
    I.   All Nassau County police officers weigh less than 225 pounds.
    II. No police officer weighs more than 225 pounds.
         No police officer is an alcoholic. No alcoholic is a police officer.
    The CORRECT answer is:

    A. I *only*   B. II *only*
    C. Both I and II   D. Neither I nor II

3. Summary of Evidence Collected to Date: All pimps in the precinct own pink-colored cars   3.____
    and carry knives.
    Prematurely Drawn Conclusion: Any person in the precinct who carries a knife is a pimp.
    Which one of the following additional pieces of evidence, if any, would make it *reasonably certain* that the conclusion drawn is TRUE?

    A. Each person who carries a knife owns a pink-colored car.
    B. All persons who own pink-colored cars pimp.

C. No one who carries a knife has a vocation other than pimping.
D. None of these

4. Summary of Evidence Collected to Date: 4.
    1. Some of the robbery suspects have served time as convicted felons.
    2. Some of the robbery suspects are female.
    Prematurely Drawn Conclusion: Some of the female suspects have never served time
    as convicted felons.
    Which one of the following additional pieces of evidence, if any, would make it *reasonably certain* that the conclusion drawn is TRUE?

    A. The number of female suspects is the same as the number of robbery suspects
        who have served time as convicted felons.
    B. The number of female suspects is smaller than the number of convicted felons.
    C. The number of suspects that have served time is smaller than the number of suspects that have been convicted of a felony.
    D. None of these

Questions 5-8.

DIRECTIONS: Questions 5 to 8 measure your ability to orient yourself within a given section
              of a town, neighborhood, or particular area. Each of the questions describes a
              starting point and a destination. Assume that you are driving a patrol car in the
              area shown on the map accompanying the questions. Use the map as a basis
              for choosing the shortest way to get from one point to another without breaking
              the law.

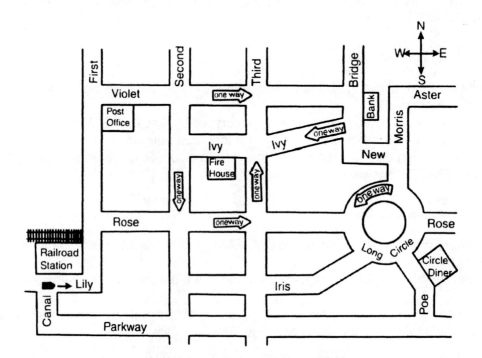

A street marked *one way* is one-way for the full length, even when there are breaks or jogs in
the street. EXCEPTION: A street that does not have the same name over the full length.

5. A patrol car at the train station is sent to the bank to investigate a robbery. The SHORT-   5.____
   EST way to get there without breaking any traffic laws is to go

    A. east on Lily, north on First, east on Rose, north on Third, and east on Ivy to bank
    B. east on Lily, north on First, east on Violet, and south on Bridge to bank
    C. south on Canal, east on Parkway, north on Poe, around Long Circle to Morris, west on New, and north on Bridge to bank
    D. south on Canal, east on Parkway, north on Third, and east on Ivy to bank

6. At the bank, the patrol car receives a call to hurry to the post office. The SHORTEST way   6.____
   to get there without breaking any traffic laws is to go

    A. west on Ivy, south on Second, west on Rose, and north on First to post office
    B. west on Ivy, south on Second, west on Rose, and south on First to post office
    C. south on Bridge, east on New, south on Morris, around Long Circle, south on Poe, west on Parkway, north on Canal, east on Lily, and north on First to post office
    D. north on Bridge, west on Violet, and south on First to post office.

7. On leaving the post office, the police officers decide to go to the Circle Diner. The   7.____
   SHORTEST way to get there without breaking any traffic laws is to go

    A. south on First, left on Rose, right on Second, left on Parkway, and right on Poe to diner
    B. south on First, left on Rose, around Long Circle, and right on Poe to diner
    C. south on First, left on Rose, right on Second, right on Iris, around Long Circle, and left on Poe to diner
    D. west on Violet, right on Bridge, right on New, right on Morris, around Long Circle, and left on Poe to diner

8. During lunch break, a fire siren sounds and the police officers rush to their patrol car and   8.____
   head for the fire-house. The SHORTEST way to get there without breaking any traffic
   laws is to go

    A. north on Poe, around Long Circle, west on Iris, north on Third, and west on Ivy to firehouse
    B. north on Poe, around Long Circle, north on Morris, west on New, north on Bridge, and west on Ivy to firehouse
    C. north on Poe, around Long Circle, west on Rose, north on Third, and west on Ivy to firehouse
    D. south on Poe, west on Parkway, north on Third, and east on Ivy to firehouse

Questions 9-13.

DIRECTIONS: Questions 9 to 13 measure your ability to understand written descriptions of events. Each question presents you with a description of an accident, a crime, or an event and asks you which of four drawings BEST represent it.

In the drawings, the following symbols are used (these symbols and their meanings will be repeated in the test):

A moving vehicle is represented by this symbol: (front) ▭ (rear)

A parked vehicle is represented by this symbol: (front) ◀ (rear)

A pedestrian or a bicyclist is represented by this symbol: •

The path and direction of travel of a vehicle or pedestrian is indicated by a solid line: ⟶

EXCEPTION: The path and direction of travel of each vehicle or person directly involved in a collision from the point of impact is indicated by a dotted line: --→

9. A driver pulling out from between two parked cars on Magic is struck by a vehicle heading east which turns left onto Maple and flees.
Which of the following depicts the accident?

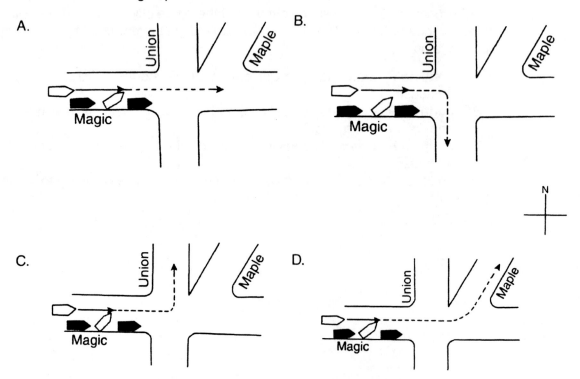

10. As Mr. Jones is driving south on Side. St., he falls asleep at the wheel. His car goes out   10._____
of control and sideswipes an oncoming car, goes through an intersection, and hits a
pedestrian on the southeast corner of Main Street.
Which of the following depicts the accident?

A.
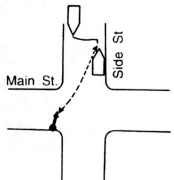

B.
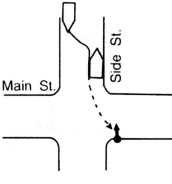

C.
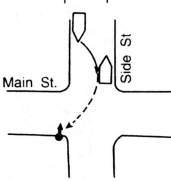

D.
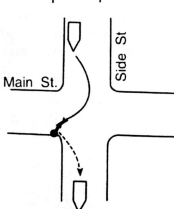

11. A car traveling south on Baltic skids through a red light at the intersection of Baltic and   11._____
Atlantic, sideswipes a car stopped for a light in the northbound lane, skids 180 degrees,
and stops on the west sidewalk of Baltic.
Which of the following depicts the accident?

A.
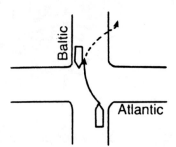

B.
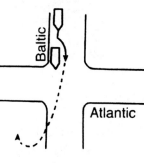

C.
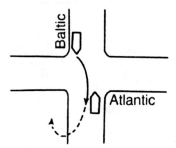

D.
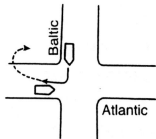

12. When found, the right front end of an automobile was smashed and bent around a post, and the hood was buckled.
Which of the following cars on a service lot is the car described?

A.

B.

C.

D.

13. An open floor safe with its door bent out of shape was found at the scene. It was empty. An electric drill and several envelopes and papers were found on the floor near the safe.
Which of the following shows the scene described?

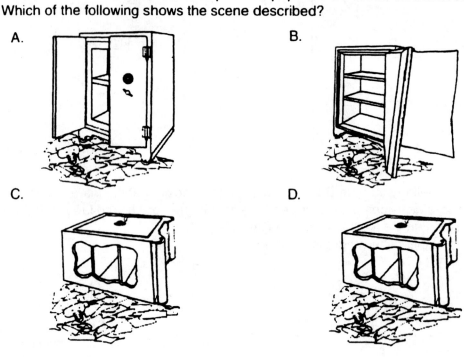

A.

B.

C.

D.

Questions 14-16.

DIRECTIONS: In Questions 14 to 16, you are to pick the word or phrase CLOSEST in meaning to the word or phrase printed in capital letters.

14. HAZARDOUS

   A. uncertain   B. threatening   C. difficult   D. dangerous

15. NEGLIGENT

   A. careless   B. fearless   C. ruthless   D. useless

16. PROVOKE

   A. accuse   B. arouse   C. insist   D. suspend

Questions 17-20.

DIRECTIONS: Questions 17 to 20 measure your ability to do arithmetic related to police work.
Each question presents a separate arithmetic problem to be solved.

17. To the nearest hour, how long can a specialized police vehicle with a 40-gallon fuel tank   17.____
be on the road before heading for a service facility, assuming that the vehicle consumes
8 gallons per hour and must head for a service facility when there are only 8 gallons in
the tank?

   A. 3   B. 4   C. 5   D.   None of these

18. A man with a history of vagrancy was found dead under a bridge with the following U.S.   18.____
currency in a band around his belly:
   7    $5   bills
   3   $10   bills
   11   $20   bills
   9   $50   bills
   4 $100   bills
What is the total amount of the money that was found in the band?

   A. $1,015   B. $1,135   C. $2,710   D.   None of these

19. X is 110 dimes.   19.____
Y is 1,111 pennies.
Which of the following statements about the values of X and Y above is TRUE?

   A.   X is greater than Y.
   B.   Y is greater than X.
   C.   X equals Y.
   D.   The relationship of X to Y cannot be determined from the information given.

20. Which of the following individuals drinking hard liquor in a bar was 21 years old at the   20.____
time of the incident?

   A.   One born August 26, 1989 - Date of incident is March 17, 2010
   B.   One born January 6, 1989 - Date of incident is New Year's Eve 2009
   C.   One born 3/17/89 - Date of incident is 2/14/10
   D.   None of these

KEY (CORRECT ANSWERS)

1.	A	11.	C
2.	B	12.	D
3.	C	13.	B
4.	D	14.	D
5.	B	15.	A
6.	C	16.	B
7.	B	17.	B
8.	B	18.	B
9.	D	19.	B
10.	B	20.	D

———

EXAMINATION SECTION
TEST 1

DIRECTIONS: Each question or incomplete statement is followed by several suggested answers or completions. Select the one that BEST answers the question or completes the statement. *PRINT THE LETTER OF THE CORRECT ANSWER IN THE SPACE AT THE RIGHT.*

Questions 1 -9

Questions 1 through 9 measure your ability to (1) determine whether statements from witnesses say essentially the same thing and (2) determine the evidence needed to make it reasonably certain that a particular conclusion is true.

1. Which of the following pairs of statements say essentially the same thing in two different ways?

    I. All Hoxie steelworkers are at least six feet tall. No steelworker is less than six feet tall.

    II. Some neutered pit bulls are not dangerous dogs. Some dangerous dogs are neutered pit bulls.

    A. I only
    B. I and II
    C. II only
    D. Neither I nor II

1.____

2. Which of the following pairs of statements say essentially the same thing in two different ways?

    I. If we are in training today, it is definitely Wednesday. Every Wednesday there is training.

    II. You may go out tonight only after you clean your room. If you clean your room, you may go out tonight.

    A. I only
    B. I and II
    C. II only
    D. Neither I nor II

2.____

3. Which of the following pairs of statements say essentially the same thing in two different ways?

    I. The case will be dismissed if either the defendant pleads guilty and agrees to perform community service, or the defendant pleads guilty and makes a full apology to the victim.
The case will be dismissed if the defendant pleads guilty and either agrees to perform community service or makes a full apology to the victim.

    II. Long books are fun to read.
Books that aren't fun to read aren't long.

    A. I only
    B. I and II
    C. II only
    D. Neither I nor II

3.____

4. Which of the following pairs of statements say essentially the same thing in two different ways?   4.___

      I.   If you live in a mansion, you have a big heating bill. If you do not have a big heating bill, you do not live in a mansion.

     II. Some clerks can both type and read shorthand. Some clerks can neither type nor read shorthand.

  A. I only
  B. I and II
  C. II only
  D. Neither I nor II

5. Summary of Evidence Collected to Date: 5.___

     I.   Three students - Bob, Mary and Stan - each received a grade of A, C and F on the civil service exam.

     II. Stan did not receive an F on the exam.

Prematurely Drawn Conclusion: Stan received an A.

Which of the following pieces of evidence, if any, would make it *reasonably certain* that the conclusion drawn is true?

  A. Bob received an F
  B. Mary received a C
  C. Bob did not receive an A
  D. None of these

6. Summary of Evidence Collected to Date: 6.___

     I.   At Walco, all the employees who work the morning shift work the evening shift as well.

     II. Some Walco employees who work the evening shift also work the afternoon shift.

Prematurely Drawn Conclusion: If Ron, a Walco employee, works the morning shift, he does not work the afternoon shift.

Which of the following pieces of evidence, if any, would make it *reasonably certain* that the conclusion drawn is true?

  A. Ron works only two shifts
  B. Ron works the evening shift
  C. All Walco employees work at least one shift
  D. None of these

7. Summary of Evidence Collected to Date: 7.___

All the family counselors at the agency have an MTF certification and an advanced degree.

Prematurely Drawn Conclusion: Any employee of the agency who has an advanced degree is a family counselor.

Which of the following pieces of evidence, if any, would make it *reasonably certain* that the conclusion drawn is true?

A. Nobody at the agency who has an advanced degree is employed as anything other than a family counselor
B. Everyone who has an MTF certification is a family counselor
C. Each person at the agency who has an MTF certification also has an advanced degree
D. None of these

8. Summary of Evidence Collected to Date: 8._____
Margery, a worker at the elder agency, is working on recreational programs.
Prematurely Drawn Conclusion: Margery is not working on cases of elder abuse.
Which of the following pieces of evidence, if any, would make it *reasonably certain* that the conclusion drawn is true?

   A. Elder abuse and recreational programs are unrelated fields
   B. Nobody at the elder agency who works on cases of elder abuse works on recreation programs
   C. Nobody at the elder agency who works on recreational programs works on cases of elder abuse
   D. None of these

9. Summary of Evidence Collected to Date: 9._____
      I.   St. Leo's Cathedral is not as tall as the FarCorp building.
      II. The FarCorp building and the Hyatt Uptown are the same height.
Prematurely Drawn Conclusion: The FarCorp building is not in Springfield.
Which of the following pieces of evidence, if any, would make it *reasonably certain* that the conclusion drawn is true?

   A. No buildings in Springfield are as tall as the Hyatt Uptown
   B. The Hyatt Uptown is not in Springfield
   C. St. Leo's Cathedral is the oldest building in Springfield
   D. None of these

Questions 10-14

Questions 10 through 14 refer to Map #1 and measure your ability to orient yourself within a given section of town, neighborhood or particular area. Each of the questions describes a starting point and a destination. Assume that you are driving a car in the area shown on the map accompanying the questions. Use the map as a basis for the shortest way to get from one point to another without breaking the law.

On the map, a street marked by arrows, or by arrows and the words "One Way," indicates one-way travel, and should be assumed to be one-way for the entire length, even when there are breaks or jogs in the street.

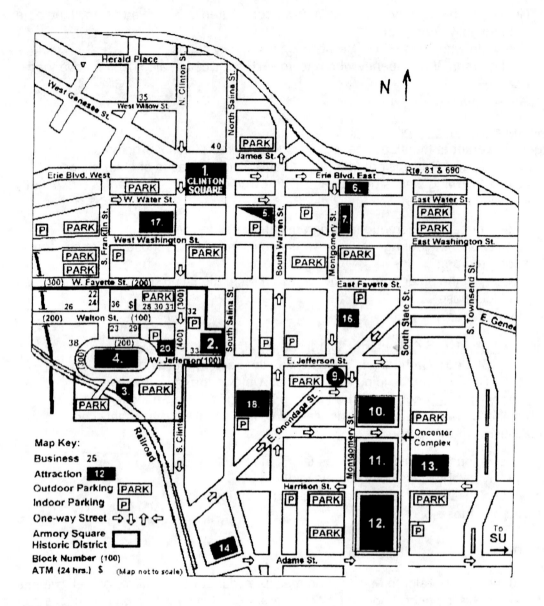

Map#1

1. Clinton Square
2. Landmark Theatre
3. OnTrack Commuter Rail Service
4. Museum of Science and Technology
5. Hanover Square
6. Erie Canal Museum
7. City Hall
9. Columbus Circle
10. Mulroy Civic Center Theaters
11. War Memorial
12. Convention Center
13. Everson Museum of Art
14. Convention and Visitors Bureau
16. Onondaga Historical Association
17. Federal Plaza
18. Galleries of Syracuse

10. The shortest legal way from Columbus Circle to Federal Plaza is   10._____

    A.   west on Jefferson St., north on Salina St., west on Water St.
    B.   east on Jefferson St., north on State St., west on Washington St.
    C.   north on Montgomery St., west on Washington St.
    D.   south on Montgomery St., west on Harrison St., north on Salina St., west on Washington St.

11. The shortest legal way from Clinton Square to the Museum of Science and Technology is   11._____

    A.   south on Clinton St., west on Fayette St., south on Franklin St.
    B.   west on Erie Blvd., south on Franklin St.
    C.   south on Clinton St., west on Water St., south on Franklin St.
    D.   south on Clinton St., west on Jefferson St.

12. The shortest legal way from Hanover Square to Landmark Theatre is   12._____

    A.   west on Water St., south on Salina St.
    B.   east on Water St., south on Montgomery St., west on Fayette St., south on Salina St.
    C.   east on Water St., south on Montgomery St., west on Fayette St., south on Clinton St., east on Jefferson St.
    D.   south on Warren St., west on Jefferson St.

13. The shortest legal way from the Convention Center to the Erie Canal Museum is   13._____

    A.   north on State St., west on Washington St., north on Montgomery St.
    B.   north on Montgomery St., jog west on Jefferson St., north on Montgomery St.
    C.   north on State St., west on Fayette St., north on Warren St., east on Water St.
    D.   north on State St., west on Water St.

14. The shortest legal way from City Hall to Clinton Square is   14._____

    A.   west on Washington St., north on Salina St.
    B.   south on Montgomery St., west on Fayette St., north on Salina St.
    C.   north on Montgomery St., west on Erie Blvd.
    D.   west on Water St.

Questions 15-19

Questions 15 through 19 refer to Figure #1, on the following page, and measure your ability to understand written descriptions of events. Each question presents a description of an accident or event and asks you which of the five drawings in Figure #1 BEST represents it.

In the drawings, the following symbols are used:

Moving vehicle: 　　　◌　　　　　Non-moving vehicle: 　　▲

Pedestrian or bicycle: 　　●

The path and direction of travel of a vehicle or pedestrian is indicated by a solid line.

The path and direction of travel of each vehicle or pedestrian directly involved in a collision from the point of impact is indicated by a dotted line.

In the space at the right, print the letter of the drawing that best fits the descriptions written below:

15. A driver heading north on Elm sideswipes a parked car, veers into the oncoming lane and travels through the intersection of Elm and Main. He then sideswipes an oncoming car, veers back into the northbound lane and flees.　　15.___

16. A driver heading south on Elm sideswipes a car parked in the southbound lane, then loses control and veers through the intersection of Elm and Main. The driver then collides with the rear of another parked car, which is knocked forward after the impact.　　16.___

17. A driver heading north on Elm strikes the rear of a parked car, which is knocked through the intersection of Elm and Main and strikes a parked car in the southbound lane head-on.　　17.___

18. A driver heading north on Elm strikes the rear of a car that is stopped at a traffic light. The car at the light is knocked through the intersection of Elm and Main and strikes a parked car in the rear.　　18.___

19. A driver heading south on Elm loses control and crosses into the other lane of traffic, where he sideswipes a car parked in the northbound lane, then veers back into the southbound lane, travels through the intersection of Elm and Main and collides with the rear end of a parked car.　　19.___

FIGURE #1

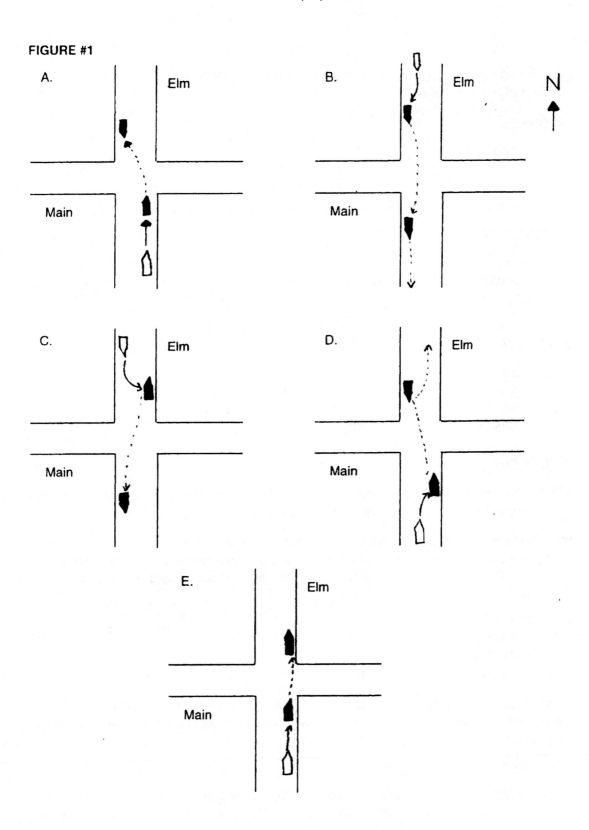

Questions 20-22

In questions 20 through 22, choose the word or phrase CLOSEST in meaning to the word or phrase printed in capital letters.

20. REDRESS

    A. suspend
    B. repeat
    C. compensate
    D. subdue

21. PRECEDENT

    A. cohort
    B. example
    C. obstruction
    D. elder

22. ADJUDICATION

    A. case
    B. judgment
    C. claim
    D. defendant

Questions 23-25

Questions 23 through 25 measure your ability to do fieldwork-related arithmetic. Each question presents a separate arithmetic problem for you to solve.

23. The Department of Sanitation purchased seven vehicles in the last year. Four of the vehicles were street sweepers that cost $95,000 each. Three were garbage compactors that cost $160,000 each. The average price of a vehicle purchased by the Department in the last year was about

    A. $98,000
    B. $108,000
    C. $122,000
    D. $145,000

24. Agent Frederick, whose car gets about 24 miles to the gallon, drives to Buffalo, 260 miles away. The average price of gasoline is $2.30 a gallon. How much did Agent Frederick spend on gas for the trip to Buffalo?

    A. $11   B. $25   C. $55   D. $113

25. Over the last four days, Precinct 11 has had 20 misdemeanor arrests each day. If the precinct records 15 misdemeanor arrests on the fifth day, what will its average daily number of misdemeanor arrests be?

    A. 16   B. 17   C. 18   D. 19

KEY (CORRECT ANSWERS)

1.	D	11.	A
2.	C	12.	B
3.	A	13.	C
4.	A	14.	A
5.	B	15.	D
6.	A	16.	B
7.	A	17.	A
8.	C	18.	E
9.	A	19.	C
10.	B	20.	C

21.	B
22.	B
23.	C
24.	B
25.	D

———————

TEST 2

Questions 1-9

Questions 1 through 9 measure your ability to (1) determine whether statements from witnesses say essentially the same thing and (2) determine the evidence needed to make it reasonably certain that a particular conclusion is true.
To do well on this part of the test, you do NOT have to have a working knowledge of police procedures and techniques. Nor do you have to have any more familiarity with criminals and criminal behavior than that acquired from reading newspapers, listening to radio or watching TV. To do well in this part, you must read and reason carefully.

1. Which of the following pairs of statements say essentially the same thing in two different ways?

    I.   All of the teachers at the school are wise, but some have proven to be bad-tempered.
        Teachers at the school are either wise or bad-tempered.

    II. If John can both type and do long division, he is qualified for this job.
        If John applies for this job, he can both type and do long division.

    A. I only
    B. I and II
    C. II only
    D. Neither I nor II

2. Which of the following pairs of statements say essentially the same thing in two different ways?

    I.   If Carl rides the A train, the C train is down.
        Carl doesn't ride the A train unless the C train is down.

    II. If the three sides of a triangle are equal, the triangle is equilateral.
        A triangle is equilateral if the three sides are equal.

    A. I only
    B. I and II
    C. II only
    D. Neither I nor II

3. Which of the following pairs of statements say essentially the same thing in two different ways?

    I.   If this dog has a red collar, it must be Slim.
        If this dog does not have a red collar, it can't be Slim.

    II. Dr. Slouka is not in his office during lunchtime.
        If it's not lunchtime, Dr. Slouka is in his office.

    A. I only
    B. I and II
    C. II only
    D. Neither I nor II

4. Which of the following pairs of statements say essentially the same thing in two different   4.____
   ways?
   I. At least one caseworker at Social Services has a degree in psychology.
       Not all the caseworkers at Social Services have a degree in psychology.
   II. If an officer doesn't pass the physical fitness test, he cannot be promoted.
       If an officer is not promoted, he hasn't passed the physical fitness test.

   A. I only   B. I and II
   C. II only   D. Neither I nor II

5. Summary of Evidence Collected to Date: 5.____
   I.   All the Class II inspectors use multiplication when they inspect escalators.
   II. On some days, Fred, a Class II inspector, doesn't use multiplication at all.
   III. Fred's friend, Garth, uses multiplication every day.
   Prematurely Drawn Conclusion: Garth inspects escalators every day.
   Which of the following pieces of evidence, if any, would make it *reasonably certain* that
   the conclusion drawn is true?

   A. Garth is a Class II inspector
   B. Fred never inspects escalators
   C. Fred usually doesn't inspect escalators
   D. None of these

6. Summary of Evidence Collected to Date: 6.____
   I. Every one of the shelter's male pit bulls has been neutered.
   II. Some male pit bulls have also been muzzled.
   Prematurely Drawn Conclusion: Rex has been neutered.
   Which of the following pieces of evidence, if any, would make it *reasonably certain* that
   the conclusion drawn is true?

   A. Rex, a pit bull at the shelter, has been muzzled
   B. All of the pit bulls at the shelter are males
   C. Rex is one of the shelter's male pit bulls
   D. None of these

7. Summary of Evidence Collected to Date: 7.____
   I. Some of the social workers at the clinic have been welfare recipients.
   II. Some of the social workers at the clinic are college graduates.
   Prematurely Drawn Conclusion: Some of the social workers at the clinic who are col-
   lege graduates have never received welfare benefits.
   Which of the following pieces of evidence, if any, would make it *reasonably certain* that
   the conclusion drawn is true?

   A. There are more college graduates at the clinic than those who have received wel-
       fare benefits
   B. There is an odd number of social workers at the clinic
   C. The number of college graduates and former welfare recipients at the clinic is the
       same
   D. None of these

8. <u>Summary of Evidence Collected to Date:</u>   8.__
    Everyone who works at the library has read *War and Peace*. Most people who have
    read *War and Peace* have also read *Anna Karenina*.
    <u>Prematurely Drawn Conclusion:</u> Marco has read *War and Peace*.
    Which of the following pieces of evidence, if any, would make it *reasonably certain* that
    the conclusion drawn is true?

    A. Marco works at the library
    B. Marco has probably read *Anna Karenina*
    C. Everyone who has read *Anna Karenina* has read *War and Peace*
    D. None of these

9. <u>Summary of Evidence Collected to Date:</u>   9.__
    Officer Skiles is working on the Martin investigation.
    <u>Prematurely Drawn Conclusion:</u> Skiles is also working on the Bartlett case.
    Which of the following pieces of evidence, if any, would make it *reasonably certain* that
    the conclusion drawn is true?

    A. Everyone who is working on the Martin investigation is also working on the Bartlett
        investigation
    B. Everyone who is working on the Bartlett investigation is also working on the Martin
        investigation
    C. The Martin investigation and Bartlett investigation are being conducted at the same
        time
    D. None of these

Questions 10-14

Questions 10 through 14 refer to Map #2 and measure your ability to orient yourself within a
given section of town, neighborhood or particular area. Each of the questions describes a starting point and a destination. Assume that you are driving a car in the area shown on the map
accompanying the questions. Use the map as a basis for the shortest way to get from one point
to another without breaking the law.

On the map, a street marked by arrows, or by arrows and the words "One Way," indicates one-
way travel, and should be assumed to be one-way for the entire length, even when there are
breaks or jogs in the street. EXCEPTION: A street that does not have the same name over the
full length.

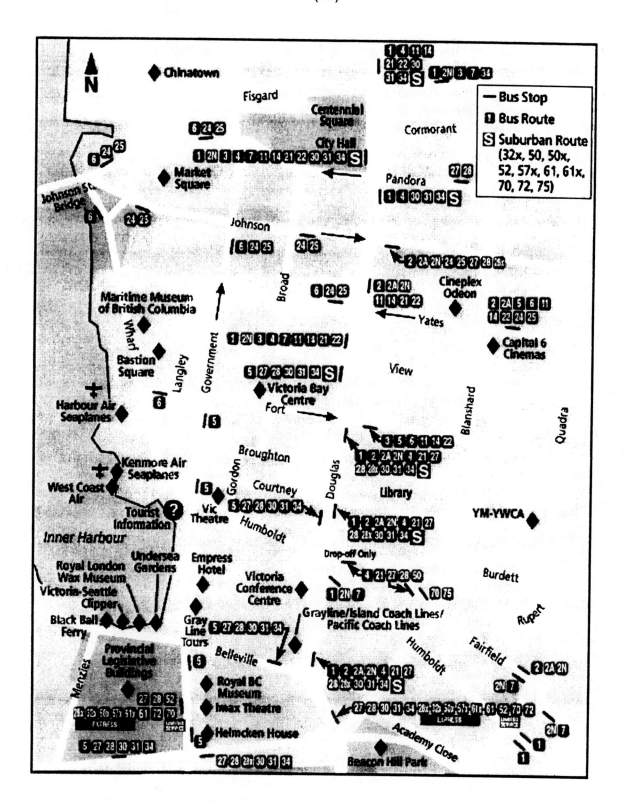

Map #2

10. The shortest legal way from the Royal London Wax Museum to the Chinatown block is   10.__

    A.   east on Belleville, north on Douglas, west on Broughton, north on Government
    B.   east on Belleville, north on Government
    C.   east on Belleville, north on Government, west on Yates, north on Wharf
    D.   east on Belleville, north on Douglas, west on Fisgard

11. The shortest legal way from the Maritime Museum of British Columbia to the Victoria Conference Centre is   11.__

    A.   north on Wharf, east on Yates, south on Douglas
    B.   south and west on Wharf, north on Government, east on Broughton, south on Douglas
    C.   south on Wharf, east on Fort, south on Douglas
    D.   south and west on Wharf, south on Government, east on Belleville, north on Douglas

12. The shortest legal way from Market Square to City Hall is   12.__

    A.   north on Government, east on Fisgard, south on Douglas
    B.   east on Pandora, north on Douglas
    C.   east on Johnson, north on Blanshard, west on Pandora, north on Douglas
    D.   east on Johnson, north on Douglas

13. The shortest legal way from the Victoria Bay Centre to Bastion Square is   13.__

    A.   east on Fort, south on Douglas, west on Broughton, north on Wharf
    B.   west on Fort, north on Government, west on Yates, south on Wharf
    C.   west on Fort, north on Wharf
    D.   east on Fort, north on Douglas, west on Johnson, south on Wharf

14. The shortest legal way from The Empress Hotel to the YM-YWCA is   14.__

    A.   north on Government, east on Broughton
    B.   north on Government, east on Courtney
    C.   north on Government, southeast on Humboldt, north on Quadra
    D.   north on Government, west on Courtney

Questions 15-19

Questions 15 through 19 refer to Figure #2, on the following page, and measure your ability to understand written descriptions of events. Each question presents a description of an accident or event and asks you which of the five drawings in Figure #2 BEST represents it.

In the drawings, the following symbols are used:

Moving vehicle: Non-moving vehicle:

Pedestrian or bicycle: ●

The path and direction of travel of a vehicle or pedestrian is indicated by a solid line.

The path and direction of travel of each vehicle or pedestrian directly involved in a collision from the point of impact is indicated by a dotted line.

In the space at the right, print the letter of the drawing that best fits the descriptions written below:

15.   A driver traveling north on Taylor strikes a parked car in the rear and knocks it forward,   15._____
      where it collides with a pedestrian in the crosswalk.

16.   A driver headed south on Taylor strikes another car that is traveling east through the   16._____
      intersection of Taylor and Hayes. After the impact, the eastbound car veers to the right
      and strikes a pedestrian in the crosswalk on Jones.

17.   A driver headed south on Taylor runs a red light and strikes another car that is headed   17._____
      east on Hayes. The eastbound car is knocked into a pedestrian that is using the cross-
      walk on Taylor

18.   A driver traveling south on Taylor makes a sudden left turn onto Hayes. In the intersec-   18._____
      tion, he strikes the front of an oncoming car and veers onto Hayes, where he strikes a
      pedestrian in the crosswalk.

19.   A driver headed west on Hayes strikes a car that is traveling east through the intersection   19._____
      of Taylor and Hayes. After the impact, the eastbound car veers to the right and strikes a
      pedestrian in the crosswalk on Jones.

FIGURE #2

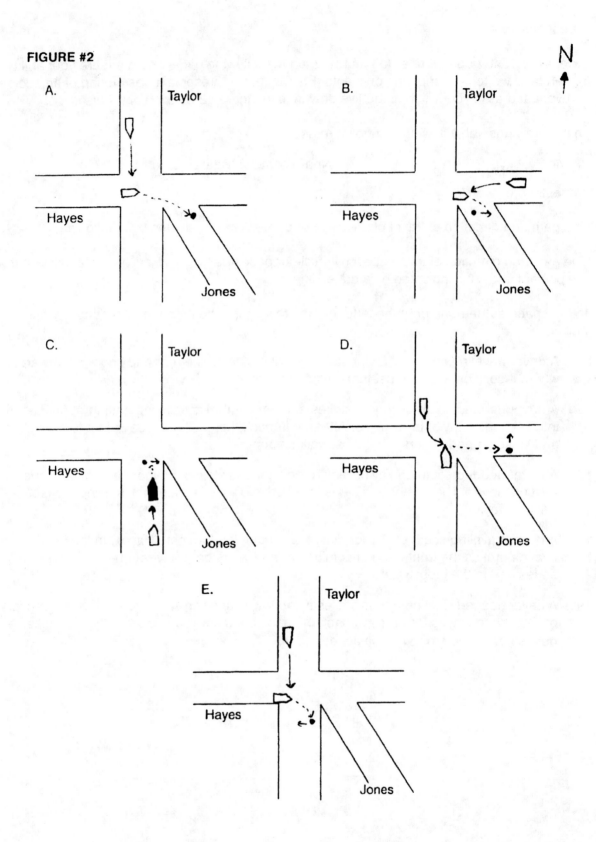

Questions 20-22

In questions 20 through 22, choose the word or phrase CLOSEST in meaning to the word or phrase printed in capital letters.

20. SEQUESTER   20.____

    A. follow
    B. separate
    C. endorse
    D. punish

21. EXECUTE   21.____

    A. carry out
    B. advance
    C. impede
    D. occur

22. SUPPRESS   22.____

    A. uphold
    B. convict
    C. forbid
    D. compensate

Questions 23-25

Questions 23 through 25 measure your ability to do fieldwork-related arithmetic. Each question presents a separate arithmetic problem for you to solve..

23. In the election for the presidency of Local Union 1134, Stan Fitz received 542 votes, Eliz- 23.____
abeth Stuckey received 430 votes and Gene Sterner received 130 votes. Ninety percent of those eligible to vote did so. What was the number of eligible voters?

    A. 900
    B. 992
    C. 1102
    D. 1224

24. The Department of Records wants to sort its files alphabetically into boxes that hold an 24.____
average of 50 files each. The Department has 1,140 records, an amount that is expected to double in the next ten years. To have enough boxes ten years from now, the Department should buy at least _____ boxes.

    A. 23   B. 38   C. 45   D. 47

25. The office's petty cash fund contains a total of $433 on Wednesday. At the beginning of 25.____
the day, Arnold reimburses $270 that he had previously borrowed from the fund. Then Janet withdraws $158 for office supplies; Hank spends $87 on lunch for a committee meeting; and at the end of the day, Ernestine buys a new office calendar for $12. How much remains in the petty cash fund at the end of the day on Wednesday?

    A. $94   B. $257   C. $446   D. $527

KEY (CORRECT ANSWERS)

1.	D		11.	C
2.	B		12.	D
3.	A		13.	A
4.	D		14.	B
5.	A		15.	C
6.	C		16.	A
7.	D		17.	E
8.	A		18.	D
9.	A		19.	B
10.	B		20.	B

21. A
22. C
23. D
24. D
25. C

Evaluating Conclusions in Light of Known Facts

EXAMINATION SECTION
TEST 1

DIRECTIONS: Each question or incomplete statement is followed by several suggested answers or completions. Select the one that BEST answers the question or completes the statement. *PRINT THE LETTER OF THE CORRECT ANSWER IN THE SPACE AT THE RIGHT.*

Questions 1-9.

DIRECTIONS: In questions 1-9, you will read a set of facts and a conclusion drawn from them. The conclusion may be valid or invalid, based on the facts—it's your task to determine the validity of the conclusion.

For each question, select the letter before the statement that BEST expresses the relationship between the given facts and the conclusion that has been drawn from them. Your choices are:
A. The facts prove the conclusion
B. The facts disprove the conclusion; or
C. The facts neither prove nor disprove the conclusion.

1. FACTS: If the supervisor retires, James, the assistant supervisor, will not be transferred to another department. James will be promoted to supervisor if he is not transferred. The supervisor retired.   1.____

   CONCLUSION: James will be promoted to supervisor.

   A. The facts prove the conclusion.
   B. The facts disprove the conclusion.
   C. The facts neither prove nor disprove the conclusion.

2. FACTS: In the town of Luray, every player on the softball team works at Luray National Bank. In addition, every player on the Luray softball team wears glasses.   2.____

   CONCLUSION: At least some of the people who work at Luray National Bank wear glasses.

   A. The facts prove the conclusion.
   B. The facts disprove the conclusion.
   C. The facts neither prove nor disprove the conclusion.

3. FACTS: The only time Henry and June go out to dinner is on an evening when they have childbirth classes. Their childbirth classes meet on Tuesdays and Thursdays.   3.____

   CONCLUSION: Henry and June never go out to dinner on Friday or Saturday.

   A. The facts prove the conclusion.
   B. The facts disprove the conclusion.
   C. The facts neither prove nor disprove the conclusion.

4. FACTS: Every player on the field hockey team has at least one bruise. Everyone on the field hockey team also has scarred knees.

    CONCLUSION: Most people with both bruises and scarred knees are field hockey players.

    A. The facts prove the conclusion.
    B. The facts disprove the conclusion.
    C. The facts neither prove nor disprove the conclusion.

4.___

5. FACTS: In the chess tournament, Lance will win his match against Jane if Jane wins her match against Mathias. If Lance wins his match against Jane, Christine will not win her match against Jane.

    CONCLUSION: Christine will not win her match against Jane if Jane wins her match against Mathias.

    A. The facts prove the conclusion.
    B. The facts disprove the conclusion.
    C. The facts neither prove nor disprove the conclusion.

5.___

6. FACTS: No green lights on the machine are indicators for the belt drive status. Not all of the lights on the machine's upper panel are green. Some lights on the machine's lower panel are green.

    CONCLUSION: The green lights on the machine's lower panel may be indicators for the belt drive status.

    A. The facts prove the conclusion.
    B. The facts disprove the conclusion.
    C. The facts neither prove nor disprove the conclusion.

6.___

7. FACTS: At a small, one-room country school, there are eight students: Amy, Ben, Carla, Dan, Elliot, Francine, Greg, and Hannah. Each student is in either the 6th, 7th, or 8th grade. Either two or three students are in each grade. Amy, Dan, and Francine are all in different grades. Ben and Elliot are both in the 7th grade. Hannah and Carl are in the same grade.

    CONCLUSION: Exactly three students are in the 7th grade.

    A. The facts prove the conclusion.
    B. The facts disprove the conclusion.
    C. The facts neither prove nor disprove the conclusion.

7.___

8. FACTS: Two married couples are having lunch together. Two of the four people are German and two are Russian, but in each couple the nationality of a spouse is not necessarily the same as the other's. One person in the group is a teacher, the other a lawyer, one an engineer, and the other a writer. The teacher is a Russian man. The writer is Russian, and her husband is an engineer. One of the people, Mr. Stern, is German.

    CONCLUSION: Mr. Stern's wife is a writer.

8.___

A. The facts prove the conclusion.
B. The facts disprove the conclusion.
C. The facts neither prove nor disprove the conclusion.

9. FACTS: The flume ride at the county fair is open only to children who are at least 36
inches tall. Lisa is 30 inches tall. John is shorter than Henry, but more than 10 inches
taller than Lisa.

CONCLUSION: Lisa is the only one who can't ride the flume ride.

A. The facts prove the conclusion.
B. The facts disprove the conclusion.
C. The facts neither prove nor disprove the conclusion.

9.____

Questions 10-17.

DIRECTIONS: Questions 10-17 are based on the following reading passage. It is not your
knowledge of the particular topic that is being tested, but your ability to reason
based on what you have read. The passage is likely to detail several proposed
courses of action and factors affecting these proposals. The reading passage
is followed by a conclusion or outcome based on the facts in the passage, or a
description of a decision taken regarding the situation. The conclusion is followed by a number of statements that have a possible connection to the conclusion. For each statement, you are to determine whether:

A. The statement proves the conclusion.
B. The statement supports the conclusion but does not prove it.
C. The statement disproves the conclusion.
D. The statement weakens the conclusion but does not disprove it.
E. The statement has no relevance to the conclusion.

Remember that the conclusion after the passage is to be accepted as the outcome of
what actually happened, and that you are being asked to evaluate the impact each statement would have had on the conclusion.

PASSAGE:

The Grand Army of Foreign Wars, a national veteran's organization, is struggling to
maintain its National Home, where the widowed spouses and orphans of deceased members
are housed together in a small village-like community. The Home is open to spouses and children who are bereaved for any reason, regardless of whether the member's death was
related to military service, but a new global conflict has led to a dramatic surge in the number
of members' deaths: many veterans who re-enlisted for the conflict have been killed in action.

The Grand Army of Foreign Wars is considering several options for handling the
increased number of applications for housing at the National Home, which has been tradition-
ally supported by membership dues. At its national convention, it will choose only one of the
following:

The first idea is a one-time $50 tax on all members, above and beyond the dues they pay
already. Since the organization has more than a million members, this tax should be sufficient

for the construction and maintenance of new housing for applicants on the existing grounds of the National Home. The idea is opposed, however, by some older members who live on fixed incomes. These members object in principle to the taxation of Grand Army members. The Grand Army has never imposed a tax on its members.

The second idea is to launch a national fund-raising drive and public relations campaign that will attract donations for the National Home. Several national celebrities are members of the organization, and other celebrities could be attracted to the cause. Many Grand Army members are wary of this approach, however: in the past, the net receipts of some fund-raising efforts have been relatively insignificant, given the costs of staging them.

A third approach, suggested by many of the younger members, is to have new applicants share some of the costs of construction and maintenance. The spouses and children would pay an up-front "enrollment" fee, based on a sliding scale proportionate to their income and assets, and then a monthly fee adjusted similarly to contribute to maintenance costs. Many older members are strongly opposed to this idea, as it is in direct contradiction to the principles on which the organization was founded more than a century ago.

The fourth option is simply to maintain the status quo, focus the organization's efforts on supporting the families who already live at the National Home, and wait to accept new applicants based on attrition.

CONCLUSION: At its annual national convention, the Grand Army of Foreign Wars votes to impose a one-time tax of $10 on each member for the purpose of expanding and supporting the National Home to welcome a larger number of applicants. The tax is considered to be the solution most likely to produce the funds needed to accommodate the growing number of applicants.

10. Actuarial studies have shown that because the Grand Army's membership consists mostly of older veterans from earlier wars, the organization's membership will suffer a precipitous decline in numbers in about five years. 10.___

  A.
  B.
  C.
  D.
  E.

11. After passage of the funding measure, a splinter group of older members appeals for the "sliding scale" provision to be applied to the tax, so that some members may be allowed to contribute less based on their income. 11.___

  A.
  B.
  C.
  D.
  E.

12. The original charter of the Grand Army of Foreign Wars specifically states that the organization will not levy any taxes or duties on its members beyond its modest annual dues. It takes a super-majority of attending delegates at the national convention to make alterations to the charter.

    A.
    B.
    C.
    D.
    E.

12.____

13. Six months before Grand Army of Foreign Wars' national convention, the Internal Revenue Service rules that because it is an organization that engages in political lobbying, the Grand Army must no longer enjoy its own federal tax-exempt status.

    A.
    B.
    C.
    D.
    E.

13.____

14. Two months before the national convention, Dirk Rockwell, arguably the country's most famous film actor, announces in a nationally televised interview that he has been saddened to learn of the plight of the National Home, and that he is going to make it his own personal crusade to see that it is able to house and support a greater number of widowed spouses and orphans in the future.

    A.
    B.
    C.
    D.
    E.

14.____

15. The Grand Army's final estimate is that the cost of expanding the National Home to accommodate the increased number of applicants will be about $61 million.

    A.
    B.
    C.
    D.
    E.

15.____

16. Just before the national convention, the federal Department of Veterans Affairs announces steep cuts in the benefits package that is currently offered to the widowed spouses and orphans of veterans.

    A.
    B.
    C.
    D.

16.____

17. After the national convention, the Grand Army of Foreign Wars begins charging a modest "start-up" fee to all families who apply for residence at the national home.   17.___

    A.

    B.

    C.

    D.

    E.

Questions 18-25.

DIRECTIONS: Questions 18-25 each provide four factual statements and a conclusion based on these statements. After reading the entire question, you will decide whether:
    A.   The conclusion is proved by statements 1-4;
    B.   The conclusion is disproved by statements 1-4; or
    C.   The facts are not sufficient to prove or disprove the conclusion.

18.   FACTUAL STATEMENTS: 18.___

    1. In the Field Day high jump competition, Martha jumped higher than Frank.
    2. Carl jumped higher than Ignacio.
    3. I gnacio jumped higher than Frank.
    4. Dan jumped higher than Carl.

CONCLUSION: Frank finished last in the high jump competition.

    A.   The conclusion is proved by statements 1-4.
    B.   The conclusion is disproved by statements 1-4.
    C.   The facts are not sufficient to prove or disprove the conclusion.

19.   FACTUAL STATEMENTS: 19.___

    1. The door to the hammer mill chamber is locked if light 6 is red.
    2. The door to the hammer mill chamber is locked only when the mill is operating.
    3. If the mill is not operating, light 6 is blue.
    4. Light 6 is blue.

CONCLUSION: The door to the hammer mill chamber is locked.

    A.   The conclusion is proved by statements 1-4.
    B.   The conclusion is disproved by statements 1-4.
    C.   The facts are not sufficient to prove or disprove the conclusion.

20. FACTUAL STATEMENTS: 20.____

   1. Ziegfried, the lion tamer at the circus, has demanded ten additional minutes of performance time during each show.
   2. If Ziegfried is allowed his ten additional minutes per show, he will attempt to teach Kimba the tiger to shoot a basketball.
   3. If Kimba learns how to shoot a basketball, then Ziegfried was not given his ten additional minutes.
   4. Ziegfried was given his ten additional minutes.

CONCLUSION: Despite Ziegfried's efforts, Kimba did not learn how to shoot a basketball.

   A.   The conclusion is proved by statements 1-4.
   B.   The conclusion is disproved by statements 1-4.
   C.   The facts are not sufficient to prove or disprove the conclusion.

21. FACTUAL STATEMENTS: 21.____

   1. If Stan goes to counseling, Sara won't divorce him.
   2. If Sara divorces Stan, she'll move back to Texas.
   3. If Sara doesn't divorce Stan, Irene will be disappointed.
   4. Stan goes to counseling.

CONCLUSION: Irene will be disappointed.

   A.   The conclusion is proved by statements 1-4.
   B.   The conclusion is disproved by statements 1-4.
   C.   The facts are not sufficient to prove or disprove the conclusion.

22. FACTUAL STATEMENTS: 22.____

   1. If Delia is promoted to district manager, Claudia will have to be promoted to team leader.
   2. Delia will be promoted to district manager unless she misses her fourth-quarter sales quota.
   3. If Claudia is promoted to team leader, Thomas will be promoted to assistant team leader.
   4. Delia meets her fourth-quarter sales quota.

CONCLUSION: Thomas is promoted to assistant team leader.

   A.   The conclusion is proved by statements 1-4.
   B.   The conclusion is disproved by statements 1-4.
   C.   The facts are not sufficient to prove or disprove the conclusion.

23. FACTUAL STATEMENTS: 23.___

1. Clone D is identical to Clone B.
2. Clone B is not identical to Clone A.
3. Clone D is not identical to Clone C.
4. Clone E is not identical to the clones that are identical to Clone B.

CONCLUSION: Clone E is identical to Clone D.

   A. The conclusion is proved by statements 1-4.
   B. The conclusion is disproved by statements 1-4.
   C. The facts are not sufficient to prove or disprove the conclusion.

24. FACTUAL STATEMENTS: 24.___

1. In the Stafford Tower, each floor is occupied by a single business.
2. Big G Staffing is on a floor between CyberGraphics and MainEvent.
3. Gasco is on the floor directly below CyberGraphics and three floors above Treehorn Audio.
4. MainEvent is five floors below EZ Tax and four floors below Treehorn Audio.

CONCLUSION: EZ Tax is on a floor between Gasco and MainEvent.

   A. The conclusion is proved by statements 1-4.
   B. The conclusion is disproved by statements 1-4.
   C. The facts are not sufficient to prove or disprove the conclusion.

25. FACTUAL STATEMENTS: 25.___

1. Only county roads lead to Nicodemus.
2. All the roads from Hill City to Graham County are federal highways.
3. Some of the roads from Plainville lead to Nicodemus.
4. Some of the roads running from Hill City lead to Strong City.

CONCLUSION: Some of the roads from Plainville are county roads.

   A. The conclusion is proved by statements 1-4.
   B. The conclusion is disproved by statements 1-4.
   C. The facts are not sufficient to prove or disprove the conclusion.

KEY (CORRECT ANSWERS)

1.	A		11.	A
2.	A		12.	D
3.	A		13.	E
4.	C		14.	D
5.	A		15.	B
6.	B		16.	B
7.	A		17.	C
8.	A		18.	A
9.	A		19.	B
10.	E		20.	A

21.	A
22.	A
23.	B
24.	A
25.	A

———

TEST 2

DIRECTIONS: Each question or incomplete statement is followed by several suggested answers or completions. Select the one that BEST answers the question or completes the statement. *PRINT THE LETTER OF THE CORRECT ANSWER IN THE SPACE AT THE RIGHT.*

Questions 1-9.

DIRECTIONS: In questions 1-9, you will read a set of facts and a conclusion drawn from them. The conclusion may be valid or invalid, based on the facts-it's your task to determine the validity of the conclusion.

For each question, select the letter before the statement that BEST expresses the relationship between the given facts and the conclusion that has been drawn from them. Your choices are:
A. The facts prove the conclusion
B. The facts disprove the conclusion; or
C. The facts neither prove nor disprove the conclusion.

1. FACTS: Some employees in the testing department are statisticians. Most of the statisti-   1.___
cians who work in the testing department are projection specialists. Tom Wilks works in
the testing department.

CONCLUSION: Tom Wilks is a statistician.

   A. The facts prove the conclusion.
   B. The facts disprove the conclusion.
   C. The facts neither prove nor disprove the conclusion.

2. FACTS: Ten coins are split among Hank, Lawrence, and Gail. If Lawrence gives his coins   2.___
to Hank, then Hank will have more coins than Gail. If Gail gives her coins to Lawrence,
then Lawrence will have more coins than Hank.

CONCLUSION: Hank has six coins.

   A. The facts prove the conclusion.
   B. The facts disprove the conclusion.
   C. The facts neither prove nor disprove the conclusion.

3. FACTS: Nobody loves everybody. Janet loves Ken. Ken loves everybody who loves   3.___
Janet.

CONCLUSION: Everybody loves Janet.

   A. The facts prove the conclusion.
   B. The facts disprove the conclusion.
   C. The facts neither prove nor disprove the conclusion.

4. FACTS: Most of the Torres family lives in East Los Angeles. Many people in East Los Angeles celebrate Cinco de Mayo. Joe is a member of the Torres family.

4.____

CONCLUSION: Joe lives in East Los Angeles.

   A. The facts prove the conclusion.
   B. The facts disprove the conclusion.
   C. The facts neither prove nor disprove the conclusion.

5. FACTS: Five professionals each occupy one story of a five-story office building. Dr. Kane's office is above Dr. Assad's. Dr. Johnson's office is between Dr. Kane's and Dr. Conlon's. Dr. Steen's office is between Dr. Conlon's and Dr. Assad's. Dr. Johnson is on the fourth story.

5.____

CONCLUSION: Dr. Kane occupies the top story.

   A. The facts prove the conclusion.
   B. The facts disprove the conclusion.
   C. The facts neither prove nor disprove the conclusion.

6. FACTS: To be eligible for membership in the Yukon Society, a person must be able to either tunnel through a snowbank while wearing only a T-shirt and shorts, or hold his breath for two minutes under water that is 50° F. Ray can only hold his breath for a minute and a half.

6.____

CONCLUSION: Ray can still become a member of the Yukon Society by tunneling through a snowbank while wearing a T-shirt and shorts.

   A. The facts prove the conclusion.
   B. The facts disprove the conclusion.
   C. The facts neither prove nor disprove the conclusion.

7. FACTS: A mark is worth five plunks. You can exchange four sharps for a tinplot. It takes eight marks to buy a sharp.

7.____

CONCLUSION: A sharp is the most valuable.

   A. The facts prove the conclusion.
   B. The facts disprove the conclusion.
   C. The facts neither prove nor disprove the conclusion.

8. FACTS: There are gibbons, as well as lemurs, who like to play in the trees at the monkey house. All those who like to play in the trees at the monkey house are fed lettuce and bananas.

8.____

CONCLUSION: Lemurs and gibbons are types of monkeys.

   A. The facts prove the conclusion.
   B. The facts disprove the conclusion.
   C. The facts neither prove nor disprove the conclusion.

9. FACTS: None of the Blackfoot tribes is a Salishan Indian tribe. Sal-ishan Indians came   9.___
from the northern Pacific Coast. All Salishan Indians live east of the Continental Divide.

CONCLUSION: No Blackfoot tribes live east of the Continental Divide.

   A. The facts prove the conclusion.
   B. The facts disprove the conclusion.
   C. The facts neither prove nor disprove the conclusion.

Questions 10-17.

DIRECTIONS: Questions 10-17 are based on the following reading passage. It is not your
knowledge of the particular topic that is being tested, but your ability to reason
based on what you have read. The passage is likely to detail several proposed
courses of action and factors affecting these proposals. The reading passage
is followed by a conclusion or outcome based on the facts in the passage, or a
description of a decision taken regarding the situation. The conclusion is followed by a number of statements that have a possible connection to the conclusion. For each statement, you are to determine whether:

   A. The statement proves the conclusion.
   B. The statement supports the conclusion but does not prove it.
   C. The statement disproves the conclusion.
   D. The statement weakens the conclusion but does not disprove it.
   E. The statement has no relevance to the conclusion.

Remember that the conclusion after the passage is to be accepted as the outcome of
what actually happened, and that you are being asked to evaluate the impact each statement would have had on the conclusion.

PASSAGE:

On August 12, Beverly Willey reported that she was in the elevator late on the previous
evening after leaving her office on the 16th floor of a large office building. In her report,
she states that a man got on the elevator at the 11th floor, pulled her off the elevator,
assaulted her, and stole her purse. Ms. Willey reported that she had seen the man in the
elevators and hallways of the building before. She believes that the man works in the
building. Her description of him is as follows: he is tall, unshaven, with wavy brown hair
and a scar on his left cheek. He walks with a pronounced limp, often dragging his left foot
behind his right.

CONCLUSION: After Beverly Willey makes her report, the police arrest a 43-year-man,
Barton Black, and charge him with her assault.

10. Barton Black is a former Marine who served in Vietnam, where he sustained shrapnel   10.___
wounds to the left side of his face and suffered nerve damage in his left leg.

   A.
   B.
   C.
   D.
   E.

11. When they arrived at his residence to question him, detectives were greeted at the door   11.____
by Barton Black, who was tall and clean-shaven.

    A.
    B.
    C.
    D.
    E.

12. Barton Black was booked into the county jail several days after Beverly Willey's assault.   12.____

    A.
    B.
    C.
    D.
    E.

13. Upon further investigation, detectives discover that Beverly Willey does not work at the   13.____
office building.

    A.
    B.
    C.
    D.
    E.

14. Upon further investigation, detectives discover that Barton Black does not work at the   14.____
office building.

    A.
    B.
    C.
    D.
    E.

15. In the spring of the following year, Barton Black is convicted of assaulting Beverly Willey   15.____
on August 11.

    A.
    B.
    C.
    D.
    E.

16. During their investigation of the assault, detectives determine that Beverly Willey was   16.____
assaulted on the 12th floor of the office building.

    A.
    B.
    C.
    D.
    E.

17. The day after Beverly Willey's assault, Barton Black fled the area and was never seen   17.__
     again.

     A.
     B.
     C.
     D.
     E.

Questions 18-25.

DIRECTIONS: Questions 18-25 each provide four factual statements and a conclusion based
              on these statements. After reading the entire question, you will decide
              whether:

              A.   The conclusion is proved by statements 1-4;
              B.   The conclusion is disproved by statements 1-4; or
              C.   The facts are not sufficient to prove or disprove the conclusion.

18. FACTUAL STATEMENTS: 18.__

     1. Among five spice jars on the shelf, the sage is to the right of the parsley.
     2. The pepper is to the left of the basil.
     3. The nutmeg is between the sage and the pepper.
     4. The pepper is the second spice from the left.

     CONCLUSION: The sage is the farthest to the right.

     A.   The conclusion is proved by statements 1-4.
     B.   The conclusion is disproved by statements 1-4.
     C.   The facts are not sufficient to prove or disprove the conclusion.

19. FACTUAL STATEMENTS: 19.__

     1. Gear X rotates in a clockwise direction if Switch C is in the OFF position
     2. Gear X will rotate in a counter-clockwise direction if Switch C is ON.
     3. If Gear X is rotating in a clockwise direction, then Gear Y will not be rotating at all.
     4. Switch C is ON.

     CONCLUSION: Gear X is rotating in a counter-clockwise direction.

     A.   The conclusion is proved by statements 1-4.
     B.   The conclusion is disproved by statements 1-4.
     C.   The facts are not sufficient to prove or disprove the conclusion.

20. FACTUAL STATEMENTS: 20.____
    1. Lane will leave for the Toronto meeting today only if Terence, Rourke, and Jackson all
       file their marketing reports by the end of the work day.
    2. Rourke will file her report on time only if Ganz submits last quarter's data.
    3. If Terence attends the security meeting, he will attend it with Jackson, and they will not
       file their marketing reports by the end of the work day.
    4. Ganz submits last quarter's data to Rourke.

    CONCLUSION: Lane will leave for the Toronto meeting today.

    A. The conclusion is proved by statements 1-4.
    B. The conclusion is disproved by statements 1-4.
    C. The facts are not sufficient to prove or disprove the conclusion.

21. FACTUAL STATEMENTS: 21.____

    1. Bob is in second place in the Boston Marathon.
    2. Gregory is winning the Boston Marathon.
    3. There are four miles to go in the race, and Bob is gaining on Gregory at the rate of
       100 yards every minute.
    4. There are 1760 yards in a mile, and Gregory's usual pace during the Boston Mara-
       thon is one mile every six minutes.

    CONCLUSION: Bob wins the Boston Marathon.

    A. The conclusion is proved by statements 1-4.
    B. The conclusion is disproved by statements 1-4.
    C. The facts are not sufficient to prove or disprove the conclusion.

22. FACTUAL STATEMENTS: 22.____

    1. Four brothers are named Earl, John, Gary, and Pete.
    2. Earl and Pete are unmarried.
    3. John is shorter than the youngest of the four.
    4. The oldest brother is married, and is also the tallest.

    CONCLUSION: Gary is the oldest brother.

    A. The conclusion is proved by statements 1-4.
    B. The conclusion is disproved by statements 1-4.
    C. The facts are not sufficient to prove or disprove the conclusion.

23. FACTUAL STATEMENTS: 23.____

    1. Brigade X is ten miles from the demilitarized zone.
    2. If General Woundwort gives the order, Brigade X will advance to the demilitarized
       zone, but not quickly enough to reach the zone before the conflict begins.
    3. Brigade Y, five miles behind Brigade X, will not advance unless General Woundwort
       gives the order.
    4. Brigade Y advances.

    CONCLUSION: Brigade X reaches the demilitarized zone before the conflict begins.

A. The conclusion is proved by statements 1-4.
B. The conclusion is disproved by statements 1-4.
C. The facts are not sufficient to prove or disprove the conclusion.

24. FACTUAL STATEMENTS: 24.___

1. Jerry has decided to take a cab from Fullerton to Elverton.
2. Chubby Cab charges $5 plus $3 a mile.
3. Orange Cab charges $7.50 but gives free mileage for the first 5 miles.
4. After the first 5 miles, Orange Cab charges $2.50 a mile.

CONCLUSION: Orange Cab is the cheaper fare from Fullerton to Elverton.

A. The conclusion is proved by statements 1-4.
B. The conclusion is disproved by statements 1-4.
C. The facts are not sufficient to prove or disprove the conclusion.

25. FACTUAL STATEMENTS: 25.___

1. Dan is never in class when his friend Lucy is absent.
2. Lucy is never absent unless her mother is sick.
3. If Lucy is in class, Sergio is in class also
4. Sergio is never in class when Dalton is absent.

CONCLUSION: If Lucy is absent, Dalton may be in class.

A. The conclusion is proved by statements 1-4.
B. The conclusion is disproved by statements 1-4.
C. The facts are not sufficient to prove or disprove the conclusion.

KEY (CORRECT ANSWERS)

1.	C		11.	E
2.	B		12.	B
3.	B		13.	D
4.	C		14.	E
5.	C		15.	A
6.	A		16.	E
7.	B		17.	C
8.	C		18.	C
9.	C		19.	A
10.	B		20.	C

21.	C
22.	A
23.	B
24.	C
25.	B

———

READING COMPREHENSION
UNDERSTANDING AND INTERPRETING WRITTEN MATERIAL
COMMENTARY

The ability to read, understand, and interpret written materials texts, publications, newspapers, orders, directions, expositions, legal passages is a skill basic to a functioning democracy and to an efficient business or viable government.

That is why almost all examinations – for beginning, middle, and senior levels – test reading comprehension, directly or indirectly.

The reading test measures how well you understand what you read. This is how it is done: You read a paragraph and several statements based on a question. From the statements, you choose the *one* statement, or answer, that is *BEST* supported by, or *BEST* matches, what is said in the paragraph.

SAMPLE QUESTIONS

DIRECTIONS: Each question has five suggested answers, lettered A, B, C, D, and E. Decide which one is the *BEST* answer. *PRINT THE LETTER OF THE CORRECT ANSWER IN THE SPACE AT THE RIGHT.*

1.   The prevention of accidents makes it necessary not only that safety devices be used to guard exposed machinery but also that mechanics be instructed in safety rules which they must follow for their own protection and that the light in the plant be adequate.
     The paragraph BEST supports the statement that industrial accidents

     A.   are always avoidable
     B.   may be due to ignorance
     C.   usually result from inadequate machinery
     D.   cannot be entirely overcome
     E.   result in damage to machinery

ANALYSIS
Remember what you have to do -
   First   -   Read the paragraph.
   Second -   Decide what the paragraph means.
   Third   -   Read the five suggested answers.
   Fourth -   Select the one answer which *BEST* matches what the paragraph says or is *BEST* supported by something in the paragraph. (Sometimes you may have to read the paragraph again in order to be sure which suggested answer is best.)
This paragraph is talking about three steps that should be taken to prevent industrial accidents:
   1.   use safety devices on machines
   2.   instruct mechanics in safety rules
   3.   provide adequate lighting

SELECTION

With this in mind, let's look at each suggested answer. Each one starts with "Industrial accidents ..."

SUGGESTED ANSWER A.

Industrial accidents (A) are always avoidable.

(The paragraph talks about how to avoid accidents but does not say that accidents are always avoidable.)

SUGGESTED ANSWER B.

Industrial accidents (B) may be due to ignorance.

(One of the steps given in the paragraph to prevent accidents is to instruct mechanics on safety rules. This suggests that lack of knowledge or ignorance of safety rules causes accidents. This suggested answer sounds like a good possibility for being the right answer.)

SUGGESTED ANSWER C.

Industrial accidents (C) usually result from inadequate machinery.

(The paragraph does suggest that exposed machines cause accidents, but it doesn't say that it is the usual cause of accidents. The word *usually* makes this a wrong answer.)

SUGGESTED ANSWER D.

Industrial accidents (D) cannot be entirely overcome.

(You may know from your own experience that this is a true statement. But that is not what the paragraph is talking about. Therefore, it is NOT the correct answer.)

SUGGESTED ANSWER E.

Industrial accidents (E) result in damage to machinery.

(This is a statement that may or may not be true, but, in any case, it is NOT covered by the paragraph.)

Looking back, you see that the one suggested answer of the five given that *BEST* matches what the paragraph says is

Industrial accidents (B) may be due to ignorance.
The *CORRECT* answer then is B.
Be sure you read *ALL* the possible answers before you make your choice. You may think that none of the five answers is really good, but choose the *BEST* one of the five.

---

2. Probably few people realize, as they drive on a concrete road, that steel is used to keep the surface flat in spite of the weight of the busses and trucks. Steel bars, deeply embedded in the concrete, provide sinews to take the stresses so that the stresses cannot crack the slab or make it wavy.
    The paragraph BEST supports the statement that a concrete road

A.   is expensive to build
B.   usually cracks under heavy weights
C.   looks like any other road
D.   is used only for heavy traffic
E.   is reinforced with other material

ANALYSIS

This paragraph is commenting on the fact that -
1.   few people realize, as they drive on a concrete road, that steel is deeply embedded
2.   steel keeps the surface flat
3.   steel bars enable the road to take the stresses without cracking or becoming wavy

SELECTION

Now read and think about the possible answers:
A.   A concrete road is expensive to build.
     (Maybe so but that is not what the paragraph is about.)
B.   A concrete road usually cracks under heavy weights.
     (The paragraph talks about using steel bars to prevent heavy weights from cracking concrete roads. It says nothing about how usual it is for the roads to crack. The word *usually* makes this suggested answer wrong.)
C.   A concrete road looks like any other road.
     (This may or may not be true. The important thing to note is that it has nothing to do with what the paragraph is about.)
D.   A concrete road is used only for heavy traffic.
     (This answer at least has something to do with the paragraph–concrete roads are used with heavy traffic but it does not say "used only.")
E.   A concrete road is reinforced with other material.
     (This choice seems to be the correct one on two counts: *First,* the paragraph does suggest that concrete roads are made stronger by embedding steel bars in them. This is another way of saying "concrete roads are reinforced with steel bars." *Second,* by the process of elimination, the other four choices are ruled out as correct answers simply because they do not apply.)

You can be sure that not all the reading questions will be so easy as these.

———————

SUGGESTIONS FOR ANSWERING READING QUESTIONS

1.   Read the paragraph carefully. Then read each suggested answer carefully. Read every word, because often one word can make the difference between a right and a wrong answer.
2.   Choose that answer which is supported in the paragraph itself. Do not choose an answer which is a correct statement unless it is based on information in the paragraph.
3.   Even though a suggested answer has many of the words used in the paragraph, it may still be wrong.
4.   Look out for words – such as *always, never, entirely, or only*–which tend to make a suggested answer wrong.

5. Answer first those questions which you can answer most easily. Then work on the other questions.
6. If you can't figure out the answer to the question, guess.

———

READING COMPREHENSION
UNDERSTANDING AND INTERPRETING WRITTEN MATERIAL
EXAMINATION SECTION
TEST 1

DIRECTIONS: Each question or incomplete statement is followed by several suggested answers or completions. Select the one that BEST answers the question or completes the statement. *PRINT THE LETTER OF THE CORRECT ANSWER IN THE SPACE AT THE RIGHT.*

Questions 1-3.

DIRECTIONS: Answer Questions 1 through 3 *SOLELY* on the basis of the following statement:
   The final step in an accident investigation is the making out of the police report. In the case of a traffic accident, the officer should go right from the scene to his office to write up the report. However, if a person was injured in the accident and taken to a hospital, the officer should visit him there before going to his office to prepare his report. This personal visit to the injured person does not mean that the office must make a physical examination; but he should make an effort to obtain a statement from the injured person or persons. If this is not possible, information should be obtained from the attending physician as to the extent of the injury. In any event, without fail, the name of the physician should be secured and the report should state the name of the physician and the fact that he told the officer that, at a certain stated time on a certain stated date, the injuries were of such and such a nature. If the injured person dies before the officer arrives at the hospital, it may be necessary to take the responsible person into custody at once.

1. When a person has been injured in a traffic accident, the one of the following actions which it is necessry for a police officer to take in connection with the accident report is to   1._____

    A. prepare the police report immediately after the accident, and then go to the hospital to speak to the victim
    B. do his utmost to verify the victim's story prior to preparing the official police report of the incident
    C. be sure to include the victim's statement in the police report in every case
    D. try to get the victim's version of the accident prior to preparing the police report

2. When one of the persons injured in a motor vehicle accident dies, the above paragraph provides that the police officer   2._____

    A. must immediately take the responsible person into custody, if the injured person is already dead when the officer appears at the scene of the accident
    B. must either arrest the responsible person or get a statement from him, if the injured person dies after arrival at the hospital
    C. may have to immediately arrest the responsible person, if the injured person dies in the hospital prior to the officer's arrival there
    D. may refrain from arresting the responsible person, but only if the responsible person is also seriously injured

3. When someone has been injured in a collision between two automobiles and is given   3.__
    medical treatment shortly thereafter by a physician, the *one* of the following actions
    which the police officer *MUST* take with regard to the physician is to

    A. obtain his name and his diagnosis of the injuries, regardless of the place where
        treatment was given
    B. obtain his approval of the portion of the police report relating to the injured person
        and the treatment given him prior to and after his arrival at the hospital
    C. obtain his name, his opinion of the extent of the person's injuries, and his signed
        statement of the treatment he gave the injured person
    D. set a certain stated time on a certain stated date for interviewing him, unless he is
        an attending physician in a hospital

Questions 4-7.

DIRECTIONS: Answer Questions 4 through 7 *SOLELY* on the basis of the following state-
              ment:
      Because of the importance of preserving physical evidence, the patrolman should not
enter a scene of a crime if it can be examined visually from one position and if no other press-
ing duty requires his presence there. However, there are some responsibilities that take precedence over preservation of evidence. Some examples are: rescue work, disarming
dangerous persons, quelling a disturbance. However, the patrolman should learn how to
accomplish these more vital tasks, while at the same time preserving as much evidence as
possible. If he finds it necessary to enter upon the scene, he should quickly study the place of
entry to learn if any evidence will suffer by his contact; then he should determine the routes to
be used in walking to the spot where his presence is required. Every place where a foot will
fall or where a hand or other part of his body will touch, should be examined with the eye.
Objects should not be touched or moved unless there is a definite and compelling reason. For
identification of most items of physical evidence at the initial investigation, it is seldom necessary to touch or move them.

4. The *one* of the following titles which is the *MOST* appropriate for the above paragraph is: 4.__

    A. Determining the Priority of Tasks at the Scene of a Crime
    B. The Principal Reasons for Preserving Evidence at the Scene of a Crime
    C. Precautions to Take at the Scene of a Crime
    D. Evidence to be Examined at the Scene of a Crime

5. When a patrolman feels that it is essential for him to enter the immediate area where a   5.__
    crime has been committed, he *should*

    A. quickly but carefully glance around to determine whether his entering the area will
        damage any evidence present
    B. remove all objects of evidence from his predetermined route in order to avoid step-
        ping on them
    C. carefully replace any object immediately if it is moved or touched by his hands or
        any other part of his body
    D. use only the usual place of entry to the scene in order to avoid disturbing any pos-
        sible clues left on rear doors and windows by the criminal

6. The one of the following which is the *LEAST* urgent duty of a police officer who has just reported to the scene of a crime is to   6._____

    A. disarm the hysterical victim of the crime who is wildly waving a loaded gun in all directions
    B. give first aid to a possible suspect who has been injured while attempting to leave the scene of the crime
    C. prevent observers from attacking and injuring the persons suspected of having committed the crime
    D. preserve from damage or destruction any evidence necessary for the proper prosecution of the case against the criminals

7. A police officer has just reported to the scene of a crime in response to a phone call. The *BEST* of the following actions for him to take with respect to objects of physical evidence present at the scene is to   7._____

    A. make no attempt to enter the crime scene if his entry will disturb any vital physical evidence
    B. map out the shortest straight path to follow in walking to the spot where the most physical evidence may be found
    C. move such objects of physical evidence as are necessary to enable him to assist the wounded victim of the crime
    D. quickly examine all objects of physical evidence in order to determine which objects may be touched and which may not

Questions 8-11.

DIRECTIONS: Answer Questions 8 through 11 *SOLELY* on the basis of the following statement:

After examining a document and comparing the characters with specimens of other handwritings, the laboratory technician may conclude that a certain individual definitely did write the questioned document. This opinion could be based on a large number of similar, as well as a small number of dissimilar but explainable, characteristics. On the other hand, if the laboratory technician concludes that the person in question did not write the questioned document, such an opinion could be based on the large number of characteristics which are dissimilar, or even on a small number which are dissimilar provided that these are of overriding significance, and despite the presence of explainable similarities. The laboratory expert is not always able to give a positive opinion. He may state that a certain individual probably did or did not write the questioned document. Such an opinion is usually the result of insufficient material, either in the questioned document or in the specimens submitted for comparison. Finally, the expert may be unable to come to any conclusion at all because of insufficient material submitted for comparison or because of improper specimens.

8. The one of the following which is the *MOST* appropriate title for the above statement is: 8._____

    A. Similar and Dissimilar Characteristics in Handwriting
    B. The Limitations of Handwriting Analysis in Identifying the Writer
    C. The Positive Identification of Suspects Through Their Handwriting
    D. The Inability to Identify an Individual Through His Handwriting

9. When a handwriting expert compares the handwriting on two separate documents and decides that they were written by the same person, his conclusions are *generally* based on the fact that

A. a large number of characteristics in both documents are dissimilar but the few similar characteristics are more important
B. all the characteristics are alike in both documents
C. similar characteristics need to be explained as to the cause for their similarity
D. most of the characteristics in both documents are alike and their few differences are readily explainable

9._

10. If a fingerprint technician carefully examines a handwritten threatening letter and compares it with specimens of handwriting made by a suspect, he would be *most likely* to decide that the suspect did *NOT* write the threatening letter when the handwriting specimens and the letter have

A. a small number of dissimilarities
B. a small number of dissimilar but explainable characteristics
C. important dissimilarities despite the fact that these may be few
D. some similar characteristics that are easily imitated or disguised

10._

11. There are instances when even a trained handwriting expert cannot decide definitely whether or not a certain document and a set of handwriting specimens were written by the same person. This inability to make a positive decision *generally* arises in situations where

A. only one document of considerable length is available for comparison with a sufficient supply of handwriting specimens
B. the limited nature of the handwriting specimens submitted restricts their comparability with the questioned document
C. the dissimilarities are not explainable
D. the document submitted for comparison does not include all the characteristics included in the handwriting specimens

11._

Questions 12-14.

DIRECTIONS: Answer Questions 12 through 14 *SOLELY* on the basis of the following statement:

In cases of drunken driving, or of disorderly conduct while intoxicated, too many times some person who had been completely under the influence of alcoholic liquor at the time of his arrest has walked out of court without any conviction just because an officer failed to make the proper observation. Many of the larger cities and counties make use of various scientific methods to determine the degree of intoxication of a person, such as breath, urine, and blood tests. Many of the smaller cities, however, do not have the facilities to make these various tests, and must, therefore, rely on the observation tests given at the scene. These consist, among other things, of noticing how the subject walked, talked, and acted. One test that is usually given at night is the eye reaction to light, which the officer gives by shining his flashlight into the eyes of the subject. The manner in which the pupils of the eyes react to the light helps to determine the sobriety of a person. If he is intoxicated, the pupils of his eyes are dilated more at night than the eyes of a sober person. Also, when a light is flashed into the eyes of a sober person, his pupils contract instantly, but in the case of a person under the influence of liquor, the pupils contract very slowly.

12. Many persons who have been arrested on a charge of driving while completely intoxi-   12.____
cated have been acquitted by a judge because the arresting officer had *neglected* to

    A. bring the driver to court while he was still under the influence of alcohol
    B. make the required scientific tests to fully substantiate his careful personal observa-
    tions of the driver's intoxicated condition
    C. submit to the court any test results showing the driver's condition or degree of
    drunkenness
    D. watch the driver closely for some pertinent facts which would support the officer's
    suspicions of the driver's intoxicated condition

13. When a person is arrested for acting in a disorderly and apparently intoxicated manner in   13.____
public, the kind of test which would fit in *BEST* with the thought of the above statement is:

    A. In many smaller cities, a close watch on his behavior and of his reactions to various
    blood and body tests
    B. In many smaller cities, having him walk a straight line
    C. In most larger counties, a close watch of the speed of his reactions to the flashlight
    test
    D. In most cities of all sizes, the application of the latest scientific techniques in the
    analysis of his breath

14. When a person suspected of driving a motor vehicle while intoxicated is being examined   14.____
to determine whether or not he actually is intoxicated, one of the methods used is to
shine the light of a flashlight into his eyes. When this method is used, the *normal* result is
that the pupils of the suspect's eyes will

    A. expand instantly if he is fully intoxicated, and remain unchanged if he is completely
    sober
    B. expand very slowly if he has had only a small amount of alcohol, and very rapidly if
    he has had a considerable amount of alcohol
    C. grow smaller at once if he is sober, and grow smaller more slowly if he is intoxi-
    cated
    D. grow smaller very slowly if he is fully sober, and grow smaller instantaneously if he
    is fully intoxicated

Questions 15-17.

DIRECTIONS: Answer Questions 15 through 17 *SOLELY* on the basis of the following statement:
    Where an officer has personal knowledge of facts, sufficient to constitute reasonable
grounds to believe that a person has committed or is committing a felony, he may arrest him,
and, after having lawfully placed him under arrest, may search and take into his possession
any incriminating evidence. The right of an officer to make an arrest and search is not limited
to cases where the officer has personal knowledge of the commission of a felony, because he
may act upon information conveyed to him by third persons which he believes to be reliable.
Where an officer, charged with the duty of enforcing the law, receives information from apparently reliable sources, which would induce in the mind of the prudent person a belief that a
felony was being or had been committed, he may make an arrest and search the person of a
defendant, but he is not justified in acting on anonymous information alone.

15. When a felony has been committed, an officer would be acting *MOST* properly if he arrested a man

    15.___

    A. when he, the officer, has a police report that the man is suspected of having been involved in several minor offenses

    B. when he, the officer, has received information from a usually reliable source that the man was involved in the crime

    C. only when he, the officer, has personal knowledge that the man has committed the felony

    D. when he, the officer, knows for a fact that the man has associated in the past with several persons who had been seen near the scene of the felony

16. An officer would be acting *MOST* properly if he searched a suspect for incriminating evidence

    16.___

    A. *when* he has received detailed information concerning the fact that the suspect is going to commit a felony

    B. *only* after having lawfully arrested the suspect and charged him with having committed a felony

    C. *when* he has just received an anonymous tip that the suspect had just committed a felony and is in illegal possession of stolen goods

    D. *in order to* find in his possession legally admissible evidence on the basis of which the officer could then proceed to arrest the suspect for having committed a felony

17. A police officer has received information from an informant that a crime has been committed. The informant has also named two persons who he says committed the crime. The officer's decision to *both* arrest and search the two suspects would be:

    17.___

    A. *Correct,* if it would not be unreasonable to assume that the crime committed is a felony, and if the informant has been trustworthy in the past

    B. *Incorrect,* if the informant has no proof but his own wdrd to offer that a felony has been committed, although he has always been trustworthy in the past

    C. *Correct,* if it would be logical and prudent to assume that the information is accurate regardless of whether the offense committed is a felony or a less serious crime

    D. *Incorrect,* even if the informant produces objective and seemingly convincing proof that a felony has been committed, but has a reputation of occasional past unreliability

Questions 18-20.

DIRECTIONS: Answer Questions 18 through 20 *SOLELY* on the basis of the following statement:

If there are many persons at the scene of a hit-and-run accident, it would be a waste of time to question all of them; the witness needed is the one who can best describe the missing auto. Usually the person most qualified to do this is a youth of fifteen or sixteen years of age. He is more likely to be able to tell the make and year of a car than most other persons. A woman may be a good witness as to how the accident occurred, but usually will be unable to tell the make of the car. As soon as any information with regard to the missing car or its description is obtained, the officer should call or radio headquarters and have the information put on the air. This should be done without waiting for further details, for time is an important factor. If a good description of the wanted car is obtained, then the next task is to get a description of the driver. In this hunt, it is found that a woman is often a more accurate witness than a man. Usually she will be able to state the color of clothes worn by the driver. If the wanted driver is a woman, another woman will often be able to tell the color and sometimes even the material of the clothing worn.

18. A hit-and-run accident has occurred and a police officer is attempting to obtain informa-   18.____
tion from persons who had witnessed the incident. It would generally be *BEST* for him to
question a

    A. boy in his late teens, when the officer is seeking an accurate description of the age,
coloring, and physical build of the driver of the car
    B. man, when the officer is seeking an accurate description of the driver of the car
and the color and material of his coat, suit,and hat
    C. woman, when the officer is seeking an accurate description of the driver of the car
    D. young teenage girl, when the officer is seeking an accurate description of the style
and color of the clothes worn by the driver of the car

19. Time is an important factor when an attempt is being made to apprehend the guilty driver   19.____
in a hit-and-run accident. However, the *EARLIEST* moment when the police should
broadcast a radio announcement of the crime is *when* a(n)

    A. description of the missing car or any facts concerning it have been obtained
    B. tentative identification of the driver of the missing car has been made
    C. detailed description of the missing car and its occupants has been obtained
    D. eyewitness account has been obtained of the accident, including the identity of the
victim, the extent of injuries, and the make and license number of the car

20. The time when it would be *MOST* desirable to get a description of the driver of the hit-   20.____
and-run car is

    A. *after* getting a description of the car itself
    B. *before* transmitting information concerning the car to headquarters for broadcast-
ing
    C. *as soon as* the officer arrives at the scene of the accident
    D. *as soon as* the victim of the accident has been given needed medical assistance

———

KEY (CORRECT ANSWERS)

1.	D		11.	B
2.	C		12.	D
3.	A		13.	B
4.	C		14.	C
5.	A		15.	B
6.	D		16.	B
7.	C		17.	A
8.	B		18.	C
9.	D		19.	A
10.	C		20.	A

———

TEST 2

Questions 1-4.

DIRECTIONS: Answer Questions 1 through 4 *SOLELY* on the basis of the following statement:

Automobile tire tracks found at the scene of a crime constitute an important link in the chain of physical evidence. In many cases, these are the only clues available. In some areas, unpaved ground adjoins the highway or paved streets. A suspect will often park his car off the paved portion of the street when committing a crime, sometimes leaving excellent tire tracks. Comparison of the tire track impressions with the tires is possible only when the vehicle has been found. However, the intial problem facing the police is the task of determining what kind of car probably made the impressions found at the scene of the crime. If the make, model,and year of the car which made the impressions can be determined, it is obvsious that the task of elimination is greatly lessened.

1. The one of the following which is the *MOST* appropriate title for the above paragraph is: 1.___

    A.   The Use of Automobiles in the Commission of Crimes
    B.   The Use of Tire Tracks in Police Work
    C.   The Capture of Criminals by Scientific Police Work
    D.   The Positive Identification of Criminals Through Their Cars

2. When searching for clear signs left by the car used in the commission of a crime, the   2.___
    MOST likely place for the police to look would be on the

    A.   highway adjoining unpaved streets
    B.   highway adjacent to paved street
    C.   paved street adjacent to the highway
    D.   unpaved ground adjacent to a highway

3. Automobile tire tracks found at the scene of a crime are of *value* as evidence in that they   3.___
    are

    A.   generally sufficient to trap and convict a suspect
    B.   the most important link in the chain of physical evidence
    C.   often the only evidence at hand
    D.   circumstantial rather than direct

4. The *PRIMARY* reason for the police to try to find out which make, model, and year of car   4.___
    was involved in the commission of a crime, is to

    A.   compare the tire tracks left at the scene of the crime with the type of tires used on
         cars of that make
    B.   determine if the mud on the tires of the suspected car matches the mud in the
         unpaved road near the scene of the crime
    C.   reduce to a large extent the amount of work involved in determining the particular
         car used in the commission of a crime
    D.   alert the police patrol forces to question the occupants of all automobiles of this
         type

Questions 5-8.

DIRECTIONS: Answer Questions 5 through 8 *SOLELY* on the basis of the following state-
                ment:

When stopping vehicles on highways to check for suspects or fugitives, the police use an
automobile roadblock whenever possible. This consists of three cars placed in prearranged
positions. Car number one is parked across the left lane of the roadway with the front diago-
nally facing toward the center line. Car number two is parked across the right lane, with the
front of the vehicle also toward the center line, in a position perpendicular to car number one
and approximately twenty feet to the rear. Continuing another twenty feet to the rear along the
highway, car number three is parked in an identical manner to car number one. The width of
the highway determines the angle or position in which the autos should be placed. In addition
to the regular roadblock signs and the use of flares at night only, there is an officer located at
both the entrance and exit to direct and control traffic from both directions. This type of roadblock forces all approaching autos to reduce speed and zigzag around the police cars. Officers standing behind the parked cars can most safely and carefully view all passing motorists.
Once a suspect is inside the block it becomes extremely difficult to crash out.

5.   Of the following, the *MOST* appropropriate title for this statement is: 5.____

     A.   The Construction of an Escape-Proof Roadblock
     B.   Regulation of Automobile Traffic Through a Police Roadblock
     C.   Safety Precautions Necessary in Making an Automobile Roadblock
     D.   Structure of a Roadblock to Detain Suspects or Fugitives

6.   When setting up a three-car roadblock, the *relative* positions of the cars should be *such*   6.____
     that

     A.   the front of car number one is placed diagonally to the center line and faces car
          number three
     B.   car number three is placed parallel to the center line and its front faces the right
          side of the road
     C.   car number two is placed about 20 feet from car number one and its front faces the
          left side of the road
     D.   car number three is parallel to and about 20 feet away from car number one

7.   Officers can observe occupants of all cars passing through the roadblock with *GREAT-*   7.____
     EST safety when

     A.   warning flares are lighted to illuminate the area sufficiently at night
     B.   warning signs are put up at each end of the roadblock
     C.   they are stationed at both the exit and the entrance of the roadblock
     D.   they take up positions behind cars in the roadblock

8.   The type of automobile roadblock described in the above paragraph is *of value* in police   8.____
     work because

     A.   a suspect is unable to escape its confines by using force
     B.   it is frequently used to capture suspects with no danger to the police
     C.   it requires only two officers to set up and operate
     D.   vehicular traffic within its confines is controled as to speed and direction

Questions 9-11.

DIRECTIONS: Answer Questions 9 through 11 *SOLELY* on the basis of the following state-
               ment:
     A problem facing the police department in one area of the city was to try to reduce the
number of bicycle thefts which had been increasing at an alarming rate in the past three or
four years. A new program was adopted to get at the root of the problem. Tags were printed,
reminding youngsters that bicycles left unlocked can be easily stolen. The police concen-
trated on such places as theaters, a municipal swimming pool, an athletic field, and the local
high school, and tied tags on all bicycles which were not locked. The majority of bicycle thefts
took place at the swimming pool. In 2006, during the first two weeks the pool was open, an
average of 10 bicycles was stolen there daily. During the same two-week period, 30 bicycles
a week were stolen at the athletic field, 15 at the high school, and 11 at all theaters combined.
In 2007, after tagging the unlocked bicycles, it was found that 20 bicycles a week were stolen
at the pool and 5 at the high school. It was felt that the police tags had helped the most,
although the school officials had helped to a great extent in this program by distributing "lock-
ing" notices to parents and children, and the use of the loudspeaker at the pool urging children to lock their bicycles had also been very helpful.

9.   The one of the following which had the *GREATEST* effect in the campaign to reduce   9.___
      bicycle stealing was the

      A.   distribution of "locking" notices by the school officials
      B.   locking of all bicycles left in public places
      C.   police tagging of bicycles left unlocked by youngsters
      D.   use of the loudspeaker at the swimming pool

10.   The tagging program was instituted by the police department *CHIEFLY* to   10.___

      A.   determine the areas where most bicycle thieves operated
      B.   instill in youngsters the importance of punishing bicycle thieves
      C.   lessen the rising rate of bicycle thefts
      D.   recover as many as possible of the stolen bicycles

11.   The figures showing the number of bicycle thefts in the various areas surveyed indicate   11.___
      that in 2006

      A.   almost as many thefts occurred at the swimming pool as at all the theaters com-
           bined
      B.   fewer thefts occurred at the athletic field than at both the high school and all the-
           aters combined
      C.   more than half the thefts occurred at the swimming pool
      D.   twice as many thefts occurred at the high school as at the athletic field

Questions 12-13.

DIRECTIONS: Answer Questions 12 and 13 *SOLELY* on the bais of the following statement:
     A survey has shown that crime prevention work is most successful if the officers are
assigned on rotating shifts to provide for around-the-clock coverage. An officer may work
days for a time and then be switched to nights. The prime object of the night work is to enable
the officer to spot conditions inviting burglars. Complete lack of, or faulty locations of, night
lights and other conditions that may invite burglars, which might go unnoticed during daylight

hours, can be located and corrected more readily through night work. Night work also enables the officer to check local hangouts of juveniles, such as bus and railway depots, certain cafes or pool halls, the local roller rink, and the building where a juvenile dance is held every Friday night. Detectives also join patrolmen cruising in radio patrol cars to check on juveniles loitering late at night and to spot-check local bars for juveniles.

12. The *MOST* important purpose of assigning officers to night shifts is to make it possible   12.____
for them to

    A.   correct conditions which may not be readily noticed during the day
    B.   discover the location of, and replace, missing and faulty night lights
    C.   locate criminal hangouts
    D.   notice things at night which cannot be noticed during the daytime

13. The type of shifting of officers which *BEST* prevents crime is to have   13.____

    A.   day-shift officers rotated to night work
    B.   rotating shifts provide sufficient officers for coverage 24 hours daily
    C.   an officer work around the clock on a 24-hour basis as police needs arise
    D.   rotating shifts to give the officers varied experience

Questions 14-15.

DIRECTIONS: Answer Questions 14 and 15 *SOLELY* on the basis of the following statement:
    Proper firearms training is one phase of law enforcement which cannot be ignored. No part of the training of a police officer is more important or more valuable. The officer's life and often the lives of his fellow officers depend directly upon his skill with the weapon he is carrying. Proficiency with the revolver is not attained exclusively by the volume of ammunition used and the number of hours spent on the firing line. Supervised practice and the use of training aids and techniques help make the shooter. It is essential to have a good firing range where new officers are trained and older personnel practice in scheduled firearms sessions. The fundamental points to be stressed are grip, stance, breathing, sight alignment and trigger squeeze. Coordination of thought, vision, and motion must be achieved before the officer gains confidence in his shooting ability. Attaining this ability will make the student a better officer and enhance his value to the force.

14. A police officer will gain confidence in his shooting ability *only after* he has   14.____

    A.   spent the required number of hours on the firing line
    B.   been given sufficient supervised practice
    C.   learned the five fundamental points
    D.   learned to coordinate revolver movement with his sight and thought

15. Proper training in the use of firearms is one aspect of law enforcement which must be   15.____
given serious consideration *CHIEFLY* because it is the

    A.   most useful and essential single factor in the training of a police officer
    B.   one phase of police officer training which stresses mental and physical coordination
    C.   costliest aspect of police officer training, involving considerable expense for the ammunition used in target practice
    D.   most difficult part of police officer training, involving the expenditure of many hours on the firing line

Questions 16-20.

DIRECTIONS: Answer Questions 16 through 20 *SOLELY* on the basis of the following statement:

Lifting consists of transferring a print that has been dusted with powder to a transfer
medium in order to preserve the print. Chemically developed prints cannot be lifted. Proper
lifting of fingerprints is difficult and should be undertaken only when other means of recording
the print are neither available nor suitable. Lifting should not be attempted from a porous surface. There are two types of commercial lifting tape which, are good transfer mediums: rubber
adhesive lift, one side of which is gummed and covered with thin, transparent celluloid; and
transparent lifting tape, made of cellophane, one side of which is gummed. A package of acetate covers, frosted on one side and used to cover and protect the lifted print, accompanies
each roll. If commercial tape is not available, transparent scotch tape may be used. The
investigator should remove the celluloid or acetate cover from the lifting tape; smooth the
tape, gummy side down, firmly and evenly over the entire print; gently peel the tape off the
surface; replace the cover; and attach pertinent identifying data to the tape. All parts of the
print should come in contact with the tape; air pockets should be avoided. The print will
adhere to the lifting tape. The cover permits the print to be viewed and protects it from damage. Transparent lifting tape does not reverse the print. If a rubber adhesive lift is utilized, the
print is reversed. Before a direct comparison can be made, the lifted print must be photo-
graphed, the negative reversed, and a positive made.

16.   An investigator wishing to preserve a record of fingerprints on a highly porous surface   16.__
should

    A.   develop them chemically before attempting to lift them
    B.   lift them with scotch tape only when no other means of recording the prints are
        available
    C.   employ some method other than lifting
    D.   dust them with powder before attempting to lift them with rubber adhesive lift

17.   Disregarding all other considerations, the *SIMPLEST* process to use in lifting a finger-   17.__
print from a window pane is *that* involving the use of

    A.   rubber adhesive lift, because it gives a positive print in one step
    B.   dusting powder and a camera, because the photograph is less likely to break than
        the window pane
    C.   a chemical process, because it both develops and preserves the print at the same
        time
    D.   transparent lifting tape, because it does not reverse the print

18.   When a piece of commercial lifting tape is being used by an investigator wishing to lift a   18.__
clear fingerprint from a smoothly-finished metal safe-door, he *should*

    A.   prevent the ends of the tape from getting stuck to the metal surface because of the
        danger of forming air-pockets and thus damaging the print
    B.   make certain that the tape covers all parts of the print and no air-pockets are
        formed
    C.   carefully roll the tape over the most significant parts of the print only to avoid form-
        ing air-pockets
    D.   be especially cautious not to destroy the air-pockets since this would tend to blur
        the print

19. When fingerprints lifted from an object found at the scene of a crime are to be compared   19.____
with the fingerprints of a suspect, the lifted print

    A. can be compared directly only if a rubber adhesive lift was used
    B. cannot be compared directly if transparent scotch tape was used
    C. can be compared directly if transparent scotch tape was used
    D. must be photographed first and a positive made if any commercial lifting tape was used

20. When a rubber adhesive lift is to be used to lift a fingerprint, the one of the following   20.____
which must be gently peeled off *FIRST* is the

    A. acetate cover   B. celluloid strip
    C. dusted surface   D. tape off the print surface

KEY (CORRECT ANSWERS)

1.	B	11.	C
2.	D	12.	A
3.	C	13.	B
4.	C	14.	D
5.	D	15.	A
6.	C	16.	C
7.	D	17.	D
8.	D	18.	B
9.	C	19.	C
10.	C	20.	B

POLICE VOCABULARY

Police officers are expected to understand and use many specialized words. Some of the words that are presented here will appear in the exam. You should know what the words mean before *you* take the test. If you have any doubt about the meaning of any of the words listed below or any other words contained in this booklet, check the definitions in a dictionary before taking the exam.

abandon	abet	accessory	accomplice
accordance	accurate	acknowledge	acquaintance
acquittal	adjacent	adjoining	admissible
advise	aid	alias	alibi
allege	allocate	altercation	annul
apparently	appearance	apprehend	apprehension
appropri ate	arson	articulate	ascertain
assailant	assume	bludgeon	boisterous
burglary	circumstances	commission	commit
complexion	competent	complaint	complainant
compliance	conceal	condone	confinement
confirm	confiscate	conjunction	constitutional
contraband	controversy	credible	corroborate
corruptible	counsel	culpable	curfew
cursory	custody	defendant	defraud
delinquent	deploy	detain	detriment
diagonally	discreet	discretion	discriminate
discriminatory	dispatch	dispatcher	disperse
disturbance	directive	dispute	divulge
duress	dwelling	effect	embezzlement
evacuation	excessive	exclude	extensive
facility	feasible	felony	frisk
fugitive	gallant	gratuities	guardian
harass	homicide	hysterical	identical
incapacitate	incarcerate	incite	incident
incriminate	indicate	indigence	influence
insufficient	interrogate	interrogation	intersecting
investigation	investigative	impede	implements
implicate	judgment	justifiable	justification
jurisdiction	juvenile	lapse	legality
loiter	malevolent	mandatory	med i ate
mi nor	misdemeanor	mitigating	negligence
negotiation	obstruct	obtain	occupant
occupation	occurrence	offender	offense
operator	pedestrian	perpetrate	perpetrator
personnel	perti nent	potential	precedence
preceding	precinct	preliminary	premeditate
premises	presence	preserve	primary
prior	priority	procedure	processing
prosecute	prosecution	prosecutor	protection
provocation	provoke	pursuant	pursuit
recovered	reinforcements	relinquish	render
request	requirement	residence	resident
respond	robbery	ruse	secure
security	seize	sequence	spontaneous
submit	subordinate	subsequent	substantial
sufficient	suspect	suspicious	suppress
technicality	technique	testify	theft
thwart	transport	vandalism	vehicle
vehicular	verify	vicinity	violate
violation	warrant		

In the test, you will be given questions like the sample questions below. For each question, you are to pick the word or phrase <u>closest</u> in meaning to the word or phrase in capital letters.

<u>SAMPLE QUESTIONS</u>

1. DIVULGE

    A. tell
    B. vomit
    C. give
    D. take

2. EXCLUDE

    A. leave out
    B. erase
    C. give to
    D. add

3. OCCUPANT

    A. job
    B. resident
    C. take over
    D. owner

KEY (CORRECT ANSWERS)

    1. A
    2. A
    3. B

EXAMINATION SECTION
TEST 1

DIRECTIONS: Each question or incomplete statement is followed by several suggested answers or completions. Select the one that BEST answers the question or completes the statement. *PRINT THE LETTER OF THE CORRECT ANSWER IN THE SPACE AT THE RIGHT.*

Questions 1-25.

DIRECTIONS: In each of Questions 1 through 25, select the lettered word or phrase which means MOST NEARLY the same as the capitalized word.

1. INTERROGATE   1._____
   A. question   B. arrest   C. search   D. rebuff

2. PERVERSE   2._____
   A. manageable   B. poetic
   C. contrary   D. patient

3. ADVOCATE   3._____
   A. champion   B. employ
   C. select   D. advise

4. APPARENT   4._____
   A. desirable   B. clear
   C. partial   D. possible

5. INSINUATE   5._____
   A. survey   B. strengthen
   C. suggest   D. insist

6. MOMENTOUS   6._____
   A. important   B. immediate   C. delayed   D. short

7. AUXILIARY   7._____
   A. exciting   B. assisting   C. upsetting   D. available

8. ADMONISH   8._____
   A. praise   B. increase   C. warn   D. polish

9. ANTICIPATE   9._____
   A. agree   B. expect   C. conceal   D. approve

10. APPREHEND   10._____
    A. confuse   B. sentence   C. release   D. seize

11. CLEMENCY   11._____
    A. silence   B. freedom   C. mercy   D. severity

12. THWART   12._____
    A. enrage   B. strike   C. choke   D. block

13. RELINQUISH   13._
    A. stretch   B. give up   C. weaken   D. flee from

14. CURTAIL   14._
    A. stop   B. reduce   C. repair   D. insult

15. INACCESSIBLE   15._
    A. obstinate   B. unreachable
    C. unreasonable   D. puzzling

16. PERTINENT   16._
    A. related   B. saucy   C. durable   D. impatient

17. INTIMIDATE   17._
    A. encourage   B. hunt   C. beat   D. frighten

18. INTEGRITY   18._
    A. honesty   B. wisdom
    C. understanding   D. persistence

19. UTILIZE   19._
    A. use   B. manufacture
    C. help   D. include

20. SUPPLEMENT   20._
    A. regulate   B. demand   C. add   D. answer

21. INDISPENSABLE   21._
    A. essential   B. neglected
    C. truthful   D. unnecessary

22. ATTAIN   22._
    A. introduce   B. spoil   C. achieve   D. study

23. PRECEDE   23._
    A. break away   B. go ahead
    C. begin   D. come before

24. HAZARD   24._
    A. penalty   B. adventure   C. handicap   D. danger

25. DETRIMENTAL   25._
    A. uncertain   B. harmful   C. fierce   D. horrible

KEY (CORRECT ANSWERS)

1.	A	6.	A	11.	C	16.	A	21.	A
2.	C	7.	B	12.	D	17.	D	22.	C
3.	A	8.	C	13.	B	18.	A	23.	D
4.	B	9.	B	14.	B	19.	A	24.	D
5.	C	10.	D	15.	B	20.	C	25.	B

TEST 2

Questions 1-20.

1. IMPLY   1.___
   - A. agree to   B. hint at   C. laugh at
   - D. mimic   E. reduce

2. APPRAISAL   2.___
   - A. allowance   B. composition   C. prohibition
   - D. quantity   E. valuation

3. DISBURSE   3.___
   - A. approve   B. expend   C. prevent
   - D. relay   E. restrict

4. POSTERITY   4.___
   - A. back payment   B. current procedure C. final effort
   - D. future generations E. rare specimen

5. PUNCTUAL   5.___
   - A. clear   B. honest   C. polite
   - D. prompt   E. prudent

6. PRECARIOUS   6.___
   - A. abundant   B. alarmed   C. cautious
   - D. insecure   E. placid

7. FOSTER   7.___
   - A. delegate   B. demote   C. encourage
   - D. plead   E. surround

8. PINNACLE   8.___
   - A. center   B. crisis   C. outcome
   - D. peak   E. personification

9. COMPONENT   9.___
   - A. flattery   B. opposite   C. part
   - D. revision   E. trend

10. SOLICIT   10.___
   - A. ask   B. prohibit   C. promise
   - D. revoke   E. surprise

11. LIAISON   11.___
    A. asset   B. coordination   C. difference
    D. policy   E. procedure

12. ALLEGE   12.___
    A. assert   B. break   C. irritate
    D. reduce   E. wait

13. INFILTRATION   13.___
    A. consumption   B. disposal   C. enforcement
    D. penetration   E. seizure

14. SALVAGE   14.___
    A. announce   B. combine   C. prolong
    D. save   E. try

15. MOTIVE   15.___
    A. attack   B. favor   C. incentive
    D. patience   E. tribute

16. PROVOKE   16.___
    A. adjust   B. incite   C. leave
    D. obtain   E. practice

17. SURGE   17.___
    A. branch   B. contract   C. revenge
    D. rush   E. want

18. MAGNIFY   18.___
    A. attract   B. demand   C. generate
    D. increase   E. puzzle

19. PREPONDERANCE   19.___
    A. decision   B. judgment   C. outweighing
    D. submission   E. warning

20. ABATE   20.___
    A. assist   B. coerce   C. diminish
    D. indulge   E. trade

Questions 21-30.

DIRECTIONS: In each of Questions 21 through 30, select the lettered word or phrase which
               means MOST NEARLY, the same as, or the opposite of, the capitalized word.

21. VINDICTIVE   21.___
    A. centrifugal   B. forgiving   C. molten
    D. tedious   E. vivacious

22. SCOPE   22.___
    A. compact   B. detriment   C. facsimile
    D. potable   E. range

23. HINDER   23.____
   - A. amplify   B. aver   C. method
   - D. observe   E. retard

24. IRATE   24.____
   - A. adhere   B. angry   C. authentic
   - D. peremptory   E. vacillate

25. APATHY   25.____
   - A. accessory   B. availability   C. fervor
   - D. pacify   E. stride

26. LUCRATIVE   26.____
   - A. effective   B. imperfect   C. injurious
   - D. timely   E. worthless

27. DIVERSITY   27.____
   - A. convection   B. slip   C. temerity
   - D. uniformity   E. viscosity

28. OVERT   28.____
   - A. laugh   B. lighter   C. orifice
   - D. quay   E. sly

29. SPORADIC   29.____
   - A. divide   B. incumbrance   C. livid
   - D. occasional   E. original

30. PREVARICATE   30.____
   - A. hesitate   B. increase   C. lie
   - D. procrastinate   E. reject

KEY (CORRECT ANSWERS)

1.	B	11.	B	21.	B
2.	E	12.	A	22.	E
3.	B	13.	D	23.	E
4.	D	14.	D	24.	B
5.	D	15.	C	25.	C
6.	D	16.	B	26.	E
7.	C	17.	D	27.	D
8.	D	18.	D	28.	E
9.	C	19.	C	29.	D
10.	A	20.	C	30.	C

TEST 3

DIRECTIONS: Each question or incomplete statement is followed by several suggested answers or completions. Select the one that BEST answers the question or completes the statement. *PRINT THE LETTER OF THE CORRECT ANSWER IN THE SPACE AT THE RIGHT.*

Questions 1-30.

DIRECTIONS: In each of Questions 1 through 30, select the lettered word which means MOST NEARLY the same as the capitalized word.

1. AVARICE 1.__
   A. flight   B. greed   C. pride   D. thrift

2. PREDATORY 2.__
   A. offensive   B. plundering
   C. previous   D. timeless

3. VINDICATE 3.__
   A. clear   B. conquer   C. correct   D. illustrate

4. INVETERATE 4.__
   A. backward   B. erect   C. habitual   D. lucky

5. DISCERN 5.__
   A. describe   B. fabricate   C. recognize   D. seek

6. COMPLACENT 6.__
   A. indulgent   B. listless   C. overjoyed   D. satisfied

7. ILLICIT 7.__
   A. insecure   B. unclear   C. unlawful   D. unlimited

8. PROCRASTINATE 8.__
   A. declare   B. multiply   C. postpone   D. steal

9. IMPASSIVE 9.__
   A. calm   B. frustrated
   C. thoughtful   D. unhappy

10. AMICABLE 10.__
    A. cheerful   B. flexible
    C. friendly   D. poised

11. FEASIBLE 11.__
    A. breakable   B. easy
    C. likeable   D. practicable

12. INNOCUOUS 12.__
    A. harmless   B. insecure
    C. insincere   D. unfavorable

13. OSTENSIBLE   13.___
   - A. apparent
   - B. hesitant
   - C. reluctant
   - D. showy

14. INDOMITABLE   14.___
   - A. excessive
   - B. unconquerable
   - C. unreasonable
   - D. unthinkable

15. CRAVEN   15.___
   - A. cowardly
   - B. hidden
   - C. miserly
   - D. needed

16. ALLAY   16.___
   - A. discuss
   - B. quiet
   - C. refine
   - D. remove

17. ALLUDE   17.___
   - A. denounce
   - B. refer
   - C. state
   - D. support

18. NEGLIGENCE   18.___
   - A. carelessness
   - B. denial
   - C. objection
   - D. refusal

19. AMEND   19.___
   - A. correct
   - B. destroy
   - C. end
   - D. list

20. RELEVANT   20.___
   - A. conclusive
   - B. careful
   - C. obvious
   - D. related

21. VERIFY   21.___
   - A. challenge
   - B. change
   - C. confirm
   - D. reveal

22. INSIGNIFICANT   22.___
   - A. incorrect
   - B. limited
   - C. unimportant
   - D. undesirable

23. RESCIND   23.___
   - A. annul
   - B. deride
   - C. extol
   - D. indulge

24. AUGMENT   24.___
   - A. alter
   - B. increase
   - C. obey
   - D. perceive

25. AUTONOMOUS   25.___
   - A. conceptual
   - B. constant
   - C. defamatory
   - D. independent

26. TRANSCRIPT   26.___
   - A. copy
   - B. report
   - C. sentence
   - D. termination

27. DISCORDANT   27.___
   - A. quarrelsome
   - B. comprised
   - C. effusive
   - D. harmonious

28. DISTEND   28.___
   - A. constrict
   - B. dilate
   - C. redeem
   - D. silence

29. EMANATE   29.___

    A. bridge   B. coherency   C. conquer   D. flow

30. EXULTANT   30.___

    A. easily upset   B. in high spirits

    C. subject to moods   D. very much over-priced

KEY (CORRECT ANSWERS)

1.	B	11.	D	21.	C
2.	B	12.	A	22.	C
3.	A	13.	A	23.	A
4.	C	14.	B	24.	B
5.	C	15.	A	25.	D
6.	D	16.	B	26.	A
7.	C	17.	B	27.	A
8.	C	18.	A	28.	B
9.	A	19.	A	29.	D
10.	C	20.	D	30.	B

PREPARING WRITTEN MATERIAL

EXAMINATION SECTION
TEST 1

DIRECTIONS: Each question or incomplete statement is followed by several suggested answers or completions. Select the one that BEST answers the question or completes the statement. *PRINT THE LETTER OF THE CORRECT ANSWER IN THE SPACE AT THE RIGHT.*

1. The one of the following sentences which is LEAST acceptable from the viewpoint of correct usage is: 1.____

   A. The police thought the fugitive to be him.
   B. The criminals set a trap for whoever would fall into it.
   C. It is ten years ago since the fugitive fled from the city.
   D. The lecturer argued that criminals are usually cowards.
   E. The police removed four bucketfuls of earth from the scene of the crime.

2. The one of the following sentences which is LEAST acceptable from the viewpoint of correct usage is: 2.____

   A. The patrolman scrutinized the report with great care.
   B. Approaching the victim of the assault, two bruises were noticed by the patrolman.
   C. As soon as I had broken down the door, I stepped into the room.
   D. I observed the accused loitering near the building, which was closed at the time.
   E. The storekeeper complained that his neighbor was guilty of violating a local ordinance.

3. The one of the following sentences which is LEAST acceptable from the viewpoint of correct usage is: 3.____

   A. I realized immediately that he intended to assault the woman, so I disarmed him.
   B. It was apparent that Mr. Smith's explanation contained many inconsistencies.
   C. Despite the slippery condition of the street, he managed to stop the vehicle before injuring the child.
   D. Not a single one of them wish, despite the damage to property, to make a formal complaint.
   E. The body was found lying on the floor.

4. The one of the following sentences which contains NO error in usage is: 4.____

   A. After the robbers left, the proprietor stood tied in his chair for about two hours before help arrived.
   B. In the cellar I found the watchmans' hat and coat.
   C. The persons living in adjacent apartments stated that they had heard no unusual noises.
   D. Neither a knife or any firearms were found in the room.
   E. Walking down the street, the shouting of the crowd indicated that something was wrong.

5. The one of the following sentences which contains NO error in usage is: 5.___

    A. The policeman lay a firm hand on the suspect's shoulder.
    B. It is true that neither strength nor agility are the most important requirement for a good patrolman.
    C. Good citizens constantly strive to do more than merely comply the restraints imposed by society.
    D. No decision was made as to whom the prize should be awarded.
    E. Twenty years is considered a severe sentence for a felony.

6. Which of the following is NOT expressed in standard English usage? 6.___

    A. The victim reached a pay-phone booth and manages to call police headquarters.
    B. By the time the call was received, the assailant had left the scene.
    C. The victim has been a respected member of the community for the past eleven years.
    D. Although the lighting was bad and the shadows were deep, the storekeeper caught sight of the attacker.
    E. Additional street lights have since been installed, and the patrols have been strengthened.

7. Which of the following is NOT expressed in standard English usage? 7.___

    A. The judge upheld the attorney's right to question the witness about the missing glove.
    B. To be absolutely fair to all parties is the jury's chief responsibility.
    C. Having finished the report, a loud noise in the next room startled the sergeant.
    D. The witness obviously enjoyed having played a part in the proceedings.
    E. The sergeant planned to assign the case to whoever arrived first.

8. In which of the following is a word misused? 8.___

    A. As a matter of principle, the captain insisted that the suspect's partner be brought for questioning.
    B. The principle suspect had been detained at the station house for most of the day.
    C. The principal in the crime had no previous criminal record, but his closest associate had been convicted of felonies on two occasions.
    D. The interest payments had been made promptly, but the firm had been drawing upon the principal for these payments.
    E. The accused insisted that his high school principal would furnish him a character reference.

9. Which of the following statements is ambiguous? 9.___

    A. Mr. Sullivan explained why Mr. Johnson had been dismissed from his job.
    B. The storekeeper told the patrolman he had made a mistake.
    C. After waiting three hours, the patients in the doctor's office were sent home.
    D. The janitor's duties were to maintain the building in good shape and to answer tenants' complaints.
    E. The speed limit should, in my opinion, be raised to sixty miles an hour on that stretch of road.

10. In which of the following is the punctuation or capitalization faulty?   10.____

    A. The accident occurred at an intersection in the Kew Gardens section of Queens, near the bus stop.
    B. The sedan, not the convertible, was struck in the side.
    C. Before any of the patrolmen had left the police car received an important message from headquarters.
    D. The dog that had been stolen was returned to his master, John Dempsey, who lived in East Village.
    E. The letter had been sent to 12 Hillside Terrace, Rutland, Vermont 05701.

Questions 11-25.

DIRECTIONS: Questions 11 through 25 are to be answered in accordance with correct English usage; that is, standard English rather than nonstandard or substandard. Nonstandard and substandard English includes words or expressions usually classified as slang, dialect, illiterate, etc., which are not generally accepted as correct in current written communication. Standard English also requires clarity, proper punctuation and capitalization and appropriate use of words. Write the letter of the sentence NOT expressed in standard English usage in the space at the right.

11. A. There were three witnesses to the accident.   11.____
    B. At least three witnesses were found to testify for the plaintiff.
    C. Three of the witnesses who took the stand was uncertain about the defendant's competence to drive.
    D. Only three witnesses came forward to testify for the plaintiff.
    E. The three witnesses to the accident were pedestrians.

12. A. The driver had obviously drunk too many martinis before leaving for home.   12.____
    B. The boy who drowned had swum in these same waters many times before.
    C. The petty thief had stolen a bicycle from a private driveway before he was apprehended.
    D. The detectives had brung in the heroin shipment they intercepted.
    E. The passengers had never ridden in a converted bus before.

13. A. Between you and me, the new platoon plan sounds like a good idea.   13.____
    B. Money from an aunt's estate was left to his wife and he.
    C. He and I were assigned to the same patrol for the first time in two months.
    D. Either you or he should check the front door of that store.
    E. The captain himself was not sure of the witness's reliability.

14. A. The alarm had scarcely begun to ring when the explosion occurred.   14.____
    B. Before the firemen arrived on the scene, the second story had been destroyed.
    C. Because of the dense smoke and heat, the firemen could hardly approach the now-blazing structure.
    D. According to the patrolman's report, there wasn't nobody in the store when the explosion occurred.
    E. The sergeant's suggestion was not at all unsound, but no one agreed with him.

15. A. The driver and the passenger they were both found to be intoxicated.
     B. The driver and the passenger talked slowly and not too clearly.
     C. Neither the driver nor his passengers were able to give a coherent account of the accident.
     D. In a corner of the room sat the passenger, quietly dozing.
     E. The driver finally told a strange and unbelievable story, which the passenger contradicted.

15.___

16. A. Under the circumstances I decided not to continue my examination of the premises.
     B. There are many difficulties now not comparable with those existing in 1960.
     C. Friends of the accused were heard to announce that the witness had better been away on the day of the trial.
     D. The two criminals escaped in the confusion that followed the explosion.
     E. The aged man was struck by the considerateness of the patrolman's offer.

16.___

17. A. An assemblage of miscellaneous weapons lay on the table.
     B. Ample opportunities were given to the defendant to obtain counsel.
     C. The speaker often alluded to his past experience with youthful offenders in the armed forces.
     D. The sudden appearance of the truck aroused my suspicions.
     E. Her studying had a good affect on her grades in high school.

17.___

18. A. He sat down in the theater and began to watch the movie.
     B. The girl had ridden horses since she was four years old.
     C. Application was made on behalf of the prosecutor to cite the witness for contempt.
     D. The bank robber, with his two accomplices, were caught in the act.
     E. His story is simply not credible.

18.___

19. A. The angry boy said that he did not like those kind of friends.
     B. The merchant's financial condition was so precarious that he felt he must avail himself of any offer of assistance.
     C. He is apt to promise more than he can perform.
     D. Looking at the messy kitchen, the housewife felt like crying.
     E. A clerk was left in charge of the stolen property.

19.___

20. A. His wounds were aggravated by prolonged exposure to sub-freezing temperatures.
     B. The prosecutor remarked that the witness was not averse to changing his story each time he was interviewed.
     C. The crime pattern indicated that the burglars were adapt in the handling of explosives.
     D. His rigid adherence to a fixed plan brought him into renewed conflict with his subordinates.
     E. He had anticipated that the sentence would be delivered by noon.

20.___

21.   A. The whole arraignment procedure is badly in need of revision.   21._____
         B. After his glasses were broken in the fight, he would of gone to the optometrist if he could.
         C. Neither Tom nor Jack brought his lunch to work.
         D. He stood aside until the quarrel was over.
         E. A statement in the psychiatrist's report disclosed that the probationer vowed to have his revenge.

22.   A. His fiery and intemperate speech to the striking employees fatally affected any   22._____
            chance of a future reconciliation.
         B. The wording of the statute has been variously construed.
         C. The defendant's attorney, speaking in the courtroom, called the official a demagogue who contempuously disregarded the judge's orders.
         D. The baseball game is likely to be the most exciting one this year.
         E. The mother divided the cookies among her two children.

23.   A. There was only a bed and a dresser in the dingy room.   23._____
         B. John is one of the few students that have protested the new rule.
         C. It cannot be argued that the child's testimony is negligible; it is, on the contrary, of the greatest importance.
         D. The basic criterion for clearance was so general that officials resolved any doubts in favor of dismissal.
         E. Having just returned from a long vacation, the officer found the city unbearably hot.

24.   A. The librarian ought to give more help to small children.   24._____
         B. The small boy was criticized by the teacher because he often wrote careless.
         C. It was generally doubted whether the women would permit the use of her apartment for intelligence operations.
         D. The probationer acts differently every time the officer visits him.
         E. Each of the newly appointed officers has 12 years of service.

25.   A. The North is the most industrialized region in the country.   25._____
         B. L. Patrick Gray 3d, the bureau's acting director, stated that, while "rehabilitation is fine" for some convicted criminals, "it is a useless gesture for those who resist every such effort."
         C. Careless driving, faulty mechanism, narrow or badly kept roads all play their part in causing accidents.
         D. The childrens' books were left in the bus.
         E. It was a matter of internal security; consequently, he felt no inclination to rescind his previous order.

KEY (CORRECT ANSWERS)

1.	C		11.	C
2.	B		12.	D
3.	D		13.	B
4.	C		14.	D
5.	E		15.	A
6.	A		16.	C
7.	C		17.	E
8.	B		18.	D
9.	B		19.	A
10.	C		20.	C

21.	B
22.	E
23.	B
24.	B
25.	D

TEST 2

DIRECTIONS: Each question or incomplete statement is followed by several suggested answers or completions. Select the one that BEST answers the question or completes the statement. *PRINT THE LETTER OF THE CORRECT ANSWER IN THE SPACE AT THE RIGHT.*

Questions 1-6.

DIRECTIONS: Each of Questions 1 through 6 consists of a statement which contains a word (one of those underlined) that is either incorrectly used because it is not in keeping with the meaning the quotation is evidently intended to convey, or is misspelled. There is only one INCORRECT word in each quotation. Of the four underlined words, determine if the first one should be replaced by the word lettered A, the second replaced by the word lettered B, the third replaced by the word lettered C, or the fourth replaced by the word lettered D. *PRINT THE LETTER OF THE REPLACEMENT WORD YOU HAVE SELECTED IN THE SPACE AT THE RIGHT.*

1. Whether one depends on <u>fluorescent</u> or artificial light or both, adequate <u>standards</u> should be <u>maintained</u> by means of <u>systematic</u> tests.

    A. natural   B. safeguards
    C. established   D. routine

1.____

2. A policeman has to be <u>prepared</u> to assume his <u>knowledge</u> as a social <u>scientist</u> in the <u>community</u>.

    A. forced   B. role
    C. philosopher   D. street

2.____

3. It is <u>practically</u> impossible to <u>indicate</u> whether a sentence is <u>too</u> long simply by <u>measuring</u> its length.

    A. almost   B. tell   C. very   D. guessing

3.____

4. Strong <u>leaders</u> are <u>required</u> to organize a community for delinquency prevention and for <u>dissemination</u> of organized <u>crime</u> and drug addiction.

    A. tactics   B. important   C. control   D. meetings

4.____

5. The <u>demonstrators</u> who were taken to the Criminal Courts building in <u>Manhattan</u> (because it was large enough to <u>accommodate</u> them), contended that the arrests were <u>unwarrented.</u>

    A. demonstraters   B. Manhatten
    C. accomodate   D. unwarranted

5.____

6. They were <u>guaranteed</u> a calm <u>atmosphere</u>, free from <u>harrassment</u>, which would be conducive to quiet consideration of the <u>indictments</u>.

    A. guarenteed   B. atmospher
    C. harassment   D. inditements

6.____

DIRECTIONS: Each of Questions 7 through 11 consists of a statement containing four words in capital letters. One of these words in capital letters is not in keeping with the meaning which the statement is evidently intended to carry. The four words in capital letters in each statement are reprinted after the statement. Print the capital letter preceding the one of the four words which does MOST to spoil the true meaning of the statement in the space at the right.

7. Retirement and pension systems are essential not only to provide employees with a   7.___
means of support in the future, but also to prevent longevity and CHARITABLE considerations from UPSETTING the PROMOTIONAL opportunities for RETIRED members of
the career service.

    A. charitable   B. upsetting
    C. promotional   D. retired

8. Within each major DIVISION in a properly set up public or private organization, provision   8.___
is made so that each NECESSARY activity is CARED for and lines of authority and
responsibility are clear-cut and INFINITE.

    A. division   B. necessary   C. cared   D. infinite

9. In public service, the scale of salaries paid must be INCIDENTAL to the services ren-   9.___
dered, with due CONSIDERATION for the attraction of the desired MANPOWER and for
the maintenance of a standard of living COMMENSURATE with the work to be performed.

    A. incidental   B. consideration
    C. manpower   D. commensurate

10. An understanding of the AIMS of an organization by the staff will AID greatly in increas- 10.___
ing the DEMAND of the correspondence work of the office, and will to a large extent
DETERMINE the nature of the correspondence.

    A. aims   B. aid   C. demand   D. determine

11. BECAUSE the Civil Service Commission strongly feels that the MERIT system is a key 11.___
factor in the MAINTENANCE of democratic government, it has adopted as one of its
major DEFENSES the progressive democratization of its own procedures in dealing with
candidates for positions in the public service.

    A. Because   B. merit
    C. maintenance   D. defenses

Questions 12-14.

DIRECTIONS: Questions 12 through 14 consist of one sentence each. Each sentence contains an incorrectly used word. First, decide which is the incorrectly used word.
Then, from among the options given, decide which word, when substituted for
the incorrectly used word, makes the meaning of the sentence clear.

<u>EXAMPLE:</u>
The U.S. national income exhibits a pattern of long term deflection.

A.	reflection	B.	subjection
C.	rejoicing	D.	growth

The word *deflection* in the sentence does not convey the meaning the sentence evidently intended to convey. The word *growth* (Answer D), when substituted for the word *deflection,* makes the meaning of the sentence clear. Accordingly, the answer to the question is D.

12. The study commissioned by the joint committee fell compassionately short of the mark and would have to be redone.   12.____

    A. successfully   B. insignificantly
    C. experimentally   D. woefully

13. He will not idly exploit any violation of the provisions of the order.   13.____

    A. tolerate   B. refuse   C. construe   D. guard

14. The defendant refused to be virile and bitterly protested service.   14.____

    A. irked   B. feasible   C. docile   D. credible

Questions 15-25.

DIRECTIONS: Questions 15 through 25 consist of short paragraphs. Each paragraph contains one word which is INCORRECTLY used because it is NOT in keeping with the meaning of the paragraph. Find the word in each paragraph which is INCORRECTLY used and then select as the answer the suggested word which should be substituted for the incorrectly used word.

<u>SAMPLE QUESTION:</u>
In determining who is to do the work in your unit, you will have to decide just who does what from day to day. One of your lowest responsibilities is to assign work so that everybody gets a fair share and that everyone can do his part well.
    A. new   B. old   C. important   D. performance

<u>EXPLANATION:</u>
The word which is NOT in keeping with the meaning of the paragraph is *lowest.* This is the INCORRECTLY used word. The suggested word *important* would be in keeping with the meaning of the paragraph and should be substituted for *lowest.* Therefore, the CORRECT answer is choice C.

15. If really good practice in the elimination of preventable injuries is to be achieved and held in any establishment, top management must refuse full and definite responsibility and must apply a good share of its attention to the task.   15.____

    A. accept   B. avoidable   C. duties   D. problem

16. Recording the human face for identification is by no means the only service performed by the camera in the field of investigation. When the trial of any issue takes place, a word picture is sought to be distorted to the court of incidents, occurrences, or events which are in dispute.   16.____

A. appeals
C. portrayed
B. description
D. deranged

17. In the collection of physical evidence, it cannot be emphasized too strongly that a hap-
hazard systematic search at the scene of the crime is vital. Nothing must be overlooked.
Often the only leads in a case will come from the results of this search.

17.___

A. important
C. proof
B. investigation
D. thorough

18. If an investigator has reason to suspect that the witness is mentally stable, or a habitual
drunkard, he should leave no stone unturned in his investigation to determine if the witness was under the influence of liquor or drugs, or was mentally unbalanced either at the
time of the occurrence to which he testified or at the time of the trial.

18.___

A. accused   B. clue   C. deranged   D. question

19. The use of records is a valuable step in crime investigation and is the main reason every
department should maintain accurate reports. Crimes are not committed through the use
of departmental records alone but from the use of all records, of almost every type, wherever they may be found and whenever they give any incidental information regarding the
criminal.

19.___

A. accidental
C. reported
B. necessary
D. solved

20. In the years since passage of the Harrison Narcotic Act of 1914, making the possession
of opium amphetamines illegal in most circumstances, drug use has become a subject of
considerable scientific interest and investigation. There is at present a voluminous litera-
ture on drug use of various kinds.

20.___

A. ingestion
C. addiction
B. derivatives
D. opiates

21. Of course, the fact that criminal laws are extremely patterned in definition does not mean
that the majority of persons who violate them are dealt with as criminals. Quite the contrary, for a great many forbidden acts are voluntarily engaged in within situations of pri-
vacy and go unobserved and unreported.

21.___

A. symbolic
C. scientific
B. casual
D. broad-gauged

22. The most punitive way to study punishment is to focus attention on the pattern of punitive
action: to study how a penalty is applied, to study what is done to or taken from an
offender.

22.___

A. characteristic
C. objective
B. degrading
D. distinguished

23. The most common forms of punishment in times past have been death, physical torture,
mutilation, branding, public humiliation, fines, forfeits of property, banishment, transportation, and imprisonment. Although this list is by no means differentiated, practically every
form of punishment has had several variations and applications.

23.___

A. specific
C. exhaustive
B. simple
D. characteristic

24. There is another important line of inference between ordinary and professional criminals, and that is the source from which they are recruited. The professional criminal seems to be drawn from legitimate employment and, in many instances, from parallel vocations or pursuits.   24.____

   A. demarcation   B. justification
   C. superiority   D. reference

25. He took the position that the success of the program was insidious on getting additional revenue.   25.____

   A. reputed   B. contingent
   C. failure   D. indeterminate

_____

KEY (CORRECT ANSWERS)

1.	A	11.	D
2.	B	12.	D
3.	B	13.	A
4.	C	14.	C
5.	D	15.	B
6.	C	16.	A
7.	D	17.	D
8.	D	18.	C
9.	A	19.	D
10.	C	20.	B

21.	D
22.	C
23.	C
24.	A
25.	B

_____

TEST 3

DIRECTIONS: Each question or incomplete statement is followed by several suggested answers or completions. Select the one that BEST answers the question or completes the statement. *PRINT THE LETTER OF THE CORRECT ANSWER IN THE SPACE AT THE RIGHT.*

Questions 1-5.

DIRECTIONS: Question 1 through 5 are to be answered on the basis of the following:

You are a supervising officer in an investigative unit. Earlier in the day, you directed Detectives Tom Dixon and Sal Mayo to investigate a reported assault and robbery in a liquor store within your area of jurisdiction.

Detective Dixon has submitted to you a preliminary investigative report containing the following information:

- At 1630 hours on 2/20, arrived at Joe's Liquor Store at 350 SW Avenue with Detective Mayo to investigate A & R.
- At store interviewed Rob Ladd, store manager, who stated that he and Joe Brown (store owner) had been stuck up about ten minutes prior to our arrival.
- Ladd described the robbers as male whites in their late teens or early twenties. Further stated that one of the robbers displayed what appeared to be an automatic pistol as he entered the store, and said, *Give us the money or we'll kill you.* Ladd stated that Brown then reached under the counter where he kept a loaded .38 caliber pistol. Several shots followed, and Ladd threw himself to the floor.
- The robbers fled, and Ladd didn't know if any money had been taken.
- At this point, Ladd realized that Brown was unconscious on the floor and bleeding from a head wound.
- Ambulance called by Ladd, and Brown was removed by same to General Hospital.
- Personally interviewed John White, 382 Dartmouth Place, who stated he was inside store at the time of occurrence. White states that he hid behind a wine display upon hearing someone say, *Give us the money.* He then heard shots and saw two young men run from the store to a yellow car parked at the curb. White was unable to further describe auto. States the taller of the two men drove the car away while the other sat on passenger side in front.
- Recovered three spent .38 caliber bullets from premises and delivered them to Crime Lab.
- To General Hospital at 1800 hours but unable to interview Brown, who was under sedation and suffering from shock and a laceration of the head.
- Alarm #12487 transmitted for car and occupants.
- Case Active.

Based solely on the contents of the preliminary investigation submitted by Detective Dixon, select one sentence from the following groups of sentences which is MOST accurate and is grammatically correct.

1. A. Both robbers were armed.
   B. Each of the robbers were described as a male white.
   C. Neither robber was armed.
   D. Mr. Ladd stated that one of the robbers was armed.

1.____

2. A. Mr. Brown fired three shots from his revolver.
   B. Mr. Brown was shot in the head by one of the robbers.
   C. Mr. Brown suffered a gunshot wound of the head during the course of the robbery.
   D. Mr. Brown was taken to General Hospital by ambulance.

2.____

3. A. Shots were fired after one of the robbers said, *Give us* the money or we'll kill you.
   B. After one of the robbers demanded the money from Mr. Brown, he fired a shot.
   C. The preliminary investigation indicated that although Mr. Brown did not have a license for the gun, he was justified in using deadly physical force.
   D. Mr. Brown was interviewed at General Hospital.

3.____

4. A. Each of the witnesses were customers in the store at the time of occurrence.
   B. Neither of the witnesses interviewed was the owner of the liquor store.
   C. Neither of the witnesses interviewed were the owner of the store.
   D. Neither of the witnesses was employed by Mr. Brown.

4.____

5. A. Mr. Brown arrived at General Hospital at about 5:00 P.M.
   B. Neither of the robbers was injured during the robbery.
   C. The robbery occurred at 3:30 P.M. on February 10.
   D. One of the witnesses called the ambulance.

5.____

Questions 6-10.

DIRECTIONS: Each of Questions 6 through 10 consists of information given in outline form and four sentences labelled A, B, C, and D. For each question, choose the one sentence which CORRECTLY expresses the information given in outline form and which also displays PROPER English usage.

6. Client's Name - Joanna Jones
   Number of Children - 3
   Client's Income - None
   Client's Marital Status - Single

   A. Joanna Jones is an unmarried client with three children who have no income.
   B. Joanna Jones, who is single and has no income, a client she has three children.
   C. Joanna Jones, whose three children are clients, is single and has no income.
   D. Joanna Jones, who has three children, is an unmarried client with no income.

6.____

7. Client's Name - Bertha Smith
   Number of Children - 2
   Client's Rent - $105 per month
   Number of Rooms - 4

7.____

A. Bertha Smith, a client, pays $105 per month for her four rooms with two children.
B. Client Bertha Smith has two children and pays $105 per month for four rooms.
C. Client Bertha Smith is paying $105 per month for two children with four rooms.
D. For four rooms and two children client Bertha Smith pays $105 per month.

8. Name of Employee - Cynthia Dawes
Number of Cases Assigned - 9
Date Cases were Assigned - 12/16
Number of Assigned Cases Completed - 8

   8.___

A. On December 16, employee Cynthia Dawes was assigned nine cases; she has completed eight of these cases.
B. Cynthia Dawes, employee on December 16, assigned nine cases, completed eight.
C. Being employed on December 16, Cynthia Dawes completed eight of nine assigned cases.
D. Employee Cynthia Dawes, she was assigned nine cases and completed eight, on December 16.

9. Place of Audit - Broadway Center
Names of Auditors - Paul Cahn, Raymond Perez
Date of Audit - 11/20
Number of Cases Audited - 41

   9.___

A. On November 20, at the Broadway Center 41 cases was audited by auditors Paul Cahn and Raymond Perez.
B. Auditors Raymond Perez and Paul Cahn has audited 41 cases at the Broadway Center on November 20.
C. At the Broadway Center, on November 20, auditors Paul Cahn and Raymond Perez audited 41 cases.
D. Auditors Paul Cahn and Raymond Perez at the Broadway Center, on November 20, is auditing 41 cases.

10. Name of Client - Barbra Levine
Client's Monthly Income - $210
Client's Monthly Expenses - $452

   10.___

A. Barbra Levine is a client, her monthly income is $210 and her monthly expenses is $452.
B. Barbra Levine's monthly income is $210 and she is a client, with whose monthly expenses are $452.
C. Barbra Levine is a client whose monthly income is $210 and whose monthly expenses are $452.
D. Barbra Levine, a client, is with a monthly income which is $210 and monthly expenses which are $452.

Questions 11-13.

DIRECTIONS: Questions 11 through 13 involve several statements of fact presented in a very simple way. These statements of fact are followed by 4 choices which attempt to incorporate all of the facts into one logical sentence which is properly constructed and grammatically correct.

11.   I.   Mr. Brown was sweeping the sidewalk in front of his house.   11.____
        II.   He was sweeping it because it was dirty.
       III. He swept the refuse into the street
      IV. Police Officer Green gave him a ticket.
   Which one of the following BEST presents the information given above?

    A. Because his sidewalk was dirty, Mr. Brown received a ticket from Officer Green when he swept the refuse into the street.
    B. Police Officer Green gave Mr. Brown a ticket because his sidewalk was dirty and he swept the refuse into the street.
    C. Police Officer Green gave Mr. Brown a ticket for sweeping refuse into the street because his sidewalk was dirty.
    D. Mr. Brown, who was sweeping refuse from his dirty sidewalk into the street, was given a ticket by Police Officer Green.

12.   I.   Sergeant Smith radioed for help.   12.____
        II.   The sergeant did so because the crowd was getting larger.
       III. It was 10:00 A.M. when he made his call.
      IV. Sergeant Smith was not in uniform at the time of occurrence.
   Which one of the following BEST presents the information given above?

    A. Sergeant Smith, although not on duty at the time, radioed for help at 10 o'clock because the crowd was getting uglier.
    B. Although not in uniform, Sergeant Smith called for help at 10:00 A.M. because the crowd was getting uglier.
    C. Sergeant Smith radioed for help at 10:00 A.M. because the crowd was getting larger.
    D. Although he was not in uniform, Sergeant Smith radioed for help at 10:00 A.M. because the crowd was getting larger.

13.   I.   The payroll office is open on Fridays.   13.____
        II.   Paychecks are distributed from 9:00 A.M. to 12 Noon.
       III. The office is open on Fridays because that's the only day the payroll staff is available.
      IV. It is open for the specified hours in order to permit employees to cash checks at the bank during lunch hour.
   The choice below which MOST clearly and accurately presents the above idea is:

    A. Because the payroll office is open on Fridays from 9:00 A.M. to 12 Noon, employees can cash their checks when the payroll staff is available.
    B. Because the payroll staff is only available on Fridays until noon, employees can cash their checks during their lunch hour.
    C. Because the payroll staff is available only on Fridays, the office is open from 9:00 A.M. to 12 Noon to allow employees to cash their checks.
    D. Because of payroll staff availability, the payroll office is open on Fridays. It is open from 9:00 A.M. to 12 Noon so that distributed paychecks can be cashed at the bank while employees are on their lunch hour.

Questions 14-16.

DIRECTIONS: In each of Questions 14 through 16, the four sentences are from a paragraph in a report. They are not in the right order. Which of the following arrangements is the BEST one?

14.   I.   An executive may answer a letter by writing his reply on the face of the letter itself instead of having a return letter typed.
   II.   This procedure is efficient because it saves the executive's time, the typist's time, and saves office file space.
   III.   Copying machines are used in small offices as well as large offices to save time and money in making brief replies to business letters.
   IV.   A copy is made on a copying machine to go into the company files, while the original is mailed back to the sender.
   The CORRECT answer is:

   A.   I, II, IV, III   B.   I, IV, II, III
   C.   III, I, IV, II   D.   III, IV, II, I

14.___

15.   I.   Most organizations favor one of the types but always include the others to a lesser degree.
   II.   However, we can detect a definite trend toward greater use of symbolic control.
   III.   We suggest that our local police agencies are today primarily utilizing material control.
   IV.   Control can be classified into three types: physical, material, and symbolic.
   The CORRECT answer is:

   A.   IV, II, III, I   B.   II, I, IV, III
   C.   III, IV, II, I   D.   IV, I, III, II

15.___

16.   I.   They can and do take advantage of ancient political and geographical boundaries, which often give them sanctuary from effective police activity.
   II.   This country is essentially a country of small police forces, each operating independently within the limits of its jurisdiction.
   III.   The boundaries that define and limit police operations do not hinder the movement of criminals, of course.
   IV.   The machinery of law enforcement in America is fragmented, complicated, and frequently overlapping.
   The CORRECT answer is:

   A.   III, I, II, IV   B.   II, IV, I, III
   C.   IV, II, III, I   D.   IV, III, II, I

16.___

17.   Examine the following sentence, and then choose from below the words which should be inserted in the blank spaces to produce the best sentence.
   The unit has exceeded _____ goals and the employees are satisfied with _____ accomplishments.

   A.   their, it's   B.   it's, it's
   C.   its, there   D.   its, their

17.___

18. Examine the following sentence, and then choose from below the words which should be   18.____
inserted in the blank spaces to produce the best sentence.
Research indicates that employees who ___ ___ no opportunity for close social rela-
tionships often find their work unsatisfying, and this _____ of satisfaction often
reflects itself in low production.

    A. have, lack   B. have, excess
    C. has, lack   D. has, excess

19. Words in a sentence must be arranged properly to make sure that the intended meaning   19.__
of the sentence is clear. The sentence below that does NOT make sense because a
clause has been separated from the word on which its meaning depends is:

    A. To be a good writer, clarity is necessary.
    B. To be a good writer, you must write clearly.
    C. You must write clearly to be a good writer.
    D. Clarity is necessary to good writing.

Questions 20-21.

DIRECTIONS: Each of Questions 20 and 21 consists of a statement which contains a word
(one of those underlined) that is either incorrectly used because it is not in
keeping with the meaning the quotation is evidently intended to convey, or is
misspelled. There is only one INCORRECT word in each quotation. Of the four
underlined words, determine if the first one should be replaced by the word lettered A, the second one replaced by the word lettered B, the third one
replaced by the word lettered C, or the fourth one replaced by the word lettered D. *PRINT THE LETTER OF THE REPLACEMENT WORD YOU HAVE
SELECTED IN THE SPACE AT THE RIGHT.*

20. The alleged killer was occasionally permitted to excercise in the corridor.   20.____

    A. alledged   B. ocasionally
    C. permited   D. exercise

21. Defense counsel stated, in affect, that their conduct was permissible under the First   21.____
Amendment.

    A. council   B. effect
    C. there   D. permissable

Question 22.

DIRECTIONS: Question 22 consists of one sentence. This sentence contains an incorrectly
used word. First, decide which is the incorrectly used word. Then, from among
the options given, decide which word, when substituted for the incorrectly used
word, makes the meaning of the sentence clear.

22. As today's violence has no single cause, so its causes have no single scheme.   22.____

    A. deference   B. cure   C. flaw   D. relevance

23. In the sentence, *A man in a light-grey suit waited thirty-five minutes in the ante-room for the all-important document,* the word IMPROPERLY hyphenated is   23.___

    A. light-grey   B. thirty-five
    C. ante-room   D. all-important

24. In the sentence, *The candidate wants to file his application for preference before it is too late,* the word *before* is used as a(n)   24.___

    A. preposition   B. subordinating conjunction
    C. pronoun   D. adverb

25. In the sentence, *The perpetrators ran from the scene,* the word *from* is a   25.___

    A. preposition   B. pronoun
    C. verb   D. conjunction

KEY (CORRECT ANSWERS)

1. D			11. D	
2. D			12. D	
3. A			13. D	
4. B			14. C	
5. D			15. D	
6. D			16. C	
7. B			17. D	
8. A			18. A	
9. C			19. A	
10. C			20. D	

           21. B
           22. B
           23. C
           24. B
           25. A

PREPARING WRITTEN MATERIAL

PARAGRAPH REARRANGEMENT
COMMENTARY

The sentences which follow are in scrambled order. You are to rearrange them in proper order and indicate the letter choice containing the correct answer at the space at the right.

Each group of sentences in this section is actually a paragraph presented in scrambled order. Each sentence in the group has a place in that paragraph; no sentence is to be left out. You are to read each group of sentences and decide upon the best order in which to put the sentences so as to form as well-organized paragraph.

The questions in this section measure the ability to solve a problem when all the facts relevant to its solution are not given.

More specifically, certain positions of responsibility and authority require the employee to discover connections between events sometimes, apparently, unrelated. In order to do this, the employee will find it necessary to correctly infer that unspecified events have probably occurred or are likely to occur. This ability becomes especially important when action must be taken on incomplete information.

Accordingly, these questions require competitors to choose among several suggested alternatives, each of which presents a different sequential arrangement of the events. Competitors must choose the MOST logical of the suggested sequences.

In order to do so, they may be required to draw on general knowledge to infer missing concepts or events that are essential to sequencing the given events. Competitors should be careful to infer only what is essential to the sequence. The plausibility of the wrong alternatives will always require the inclusion of unlikely events or of additional chains of events which are NOT essential to sequencing the given events.

It's very important to remember that you are looking for the best of the four possible choices, and that the best choice of all may not even be one of the answers you're given to choose from.

There is no one right way to these problems. Many people have found it helpful to first write out the order of the sentences, as they would have arranged them, on their scrap paper before looking at the possible answers. If their optimum answer is there, this can save them some time. If it isn't, this method can still give insight into solving the problem. Others find it most helpful to just go through each of the possible choices, contrasting each as they go along. You should use whatever method feels comfortable, and works, for you.

While most of these types of questions are not that difficult, we've added a higher percentage of the difficult type, just to give you more practice. Usually there are only one or two questions on this section that contain such subtle distinctions that you're unable to answer confidently, and you then may find yourself stuck deciding between two possible choices, neither of which you're sure about.

———

EXAMINATION SECTION
TEST 1

DIRECTIONS: The sentences that follow are in scrambled order. You are to rearrange them in proper order and indicate the letter choice containing the CORRECT answer. *PRINT THE LETTER OF THE CORRECT ANSWER IN THE SPACE AT THE RIGHT.*

1. Police Officer Jenner responds to the scene of a burglary at 2106 La Vista Boulevard. He is approached by an elderly man named Richard Jenkins, whose account of the incident includes the following five sentences:
    I. I saw that the lock on my apartment door had been smashed and the door was open.
    II. My apartment was a shambles; my belongings were everywhere and my television set was missing.
    III. As I walked down the hallway toward the bedroom, I heard someone opening a window.
    IV. I left work at 5:30 P.M. and took the bus home.
    V. At that time, I called the police.
The MOST logical order for the above sentences to appear in the report is

    A. I, V, IV, II, III   B. IV, I, II, III, V
    C. I, V, II, III, IV   D. IV, III, II, V, I

1.____

2. Police Officer LaJolla is writing an Incident Report in which back-up assistance was required. The report will contain the following five sentences:
    I. The radio dispatcher asked what my location was and he then dispatched patrol cars for back-up assistance.
    II. At approximately 9:30 P.M., while I was walking my assigned footpost, a gunman fired three shots at me.
    III. I quickly turned around and saw a white male, approximately 5'10", with black hair, wearing blue jeans, a yellow T-shirt, and white sneakers, running across the avenue carrying a handgun.
    IV. When the back-up officers arrived, we searched the area but could not find the suspect.
    V. I advised the radio dispatcher that a gunman had just fired a gun at me, and then I gave the dispatcher a description of the man.
The MOST logical order for the above sentences to appear in the report is

    A. III, V, II, IV, I   B. II, III, V, I, IV
    C. III, II, IV, I, V   D. II, V, I, III, IV

2.____

3. Police Officer Durant is completing a report of a robbery and assault. The report will contain the following five sentences:
    I. I went to Mount Snow Hospital to interview a man who was attacked and robbed of his wallet earlier that night.
    II. An ambulance arrived at 82nd Street and 3rd Avenue and took an intoxicated, wounded man to Mount Snow Hospital.
    III. Two youths attacked the man and stole his wallet.
    IV. A well-dressed man left Hanratty's Bar very drunk, with his wallet hanging out of his back pocket.
    V. A passerby dialed 911 and requested police and ambulance assistance.

3.____

The MOST logical order for the above sentences to appear in the report is

A. I, II, IV, III, V
C. IV, V, II, III, I

B. IV, III, V, II, I
D. V, IV, III, II, I

4. Police Officer Boswell is preparing a report of an armed robbery and assault which will contain the following five sentences:

    I. Both men approached the bartender and one of them drew a gun.
    II. The bartender immediately went to grab the phone at the bar.
    III. One of the men leaped over the counter and smashed a bottle over the bartender's head.
    IV. Two men in a blue Buick drove up to the bar and went inside.
    V. I found the cash register empty and the bartender unconscious on the floor, with the phone still dangling off the hook.

The MOST logical order for the above sentences to appear in the report is

A. IV, I, II, III, V
C. IV, III, II, V, I

B. V, IV, III, I, II
D. II, I, III, IV, V

5. Police Officer Mitzler is preparing a report of a bank robbery, which will contain the following five sentences:

    I. The teller complied with the instructions on the note, but also hit the silent alarm.
    II. The perpetrator then fled south on Broadway.
    III. A suspicious male entered the bank at approximately 10:45 A.M.
    IV. At this time, an undetermined amount of money has been taken.
    V. He approached the teller on the far right side and handed her a note.

The MOST logical order for the above sentences to appear in the report is

A. III, V, I, II, IV
C. III, V, IV, I, II

B. I, III, V, II, IV
D. III, V, II, IV, I

6. A Police Officer is preparing an Accident Report for an accident which occurred at the intersection of East 119th Street and Lexington Avenue. The report will include the following five sentences:

    I. On September 18, 1990, while driving ten children to school, a school bus driver passed out.
    II. Upon arriving at the scene, I notified the dispatcher to send an ambulance.
    III. I notified the parents of each child once I got to the station house.
    IV. He said the school bus, while traveling west on East 119th Street, struck a parked Ford which was on the southwest corner of East 119th Street.
    V. A witness by the name of John Ramos came up to me to describe what happened.

The MOST logical order for the above sentences to appear in the Accident Report is

A. I, II, V, III, IV
C. II, V, I, III, IV

B. I, II, V, IV, III
D. II, V, I, IV, III

7. A Police Officer is preparing a report concerning a dispute. The report will contain the following five sentences: 7._____

    I. The passenger got out of the back of the taxi and leaned through the front window to complain to the driver about the fare.

    II. The driver of the taxi caught up with the passenger and knocked him to the ground; the passenger then kicked the driver and a scuffle ensued.

    III. The taxi drew up in front of the high-rise building and stopped.

    IV. The driver got out of the taxi and followed the passenger into the lobby of the apartment building.

    V. The doorman tried but was unable to break up the fight, at which point he called the precinct.

The MOST logical order for the above sentences to appear in the report is

    A. III, I, IV, II, V   B. III, IV, I, II, V
    C. III, IV, II, V, I   D. V, I, III, IV, II

8. Police Officer Morrow is writing an Incident Report. The report will include the following four sentences: 8._____

    I. The man reached into his pocket and pulled out a gun.

    II. While on foot patrol, I identified a suspect, who was wanted for six robberies in the area, from a wanted picture I was carrying.

    III. I drew my weapon and fired six rounds at the suspect, killing him instantly.

    IV. I called for back-up assistance and told the man to put his hands up.

The MOST logical order for the above sentences to appear in the report is

    A. II, III, IV, I   B. IV, I, III, II
    C. IV, I, II, III   D. II, IV, I, III

9. Sergeant Allen responds to a call at 16 Grove Street regarding a missing child. At the scene, the Sergeant is met by Police Officer Samuels, who gives a brief account of the incident consisting of the following five sentences: 9._____

    I. I transmitted the description and waited for you to arrive before I began searching the area.

    II. Mrs. Banks, the mother, reports that she last saw her daughter Julie about 7:30 A.M. when she took her to school.

    III. About 6 P.M., my partner and I arrived at this location to investigate a report of a missing 8 year-old girl.

    IV. When Mrs. Banks left her, Julie was wearing a red and white striped T-shirt, blue jeans, and white sneakers.

    V. Mrs. Banks dropped her off in front of the playground of P.S. 11.

The MOST logical order for the above sentences to appear in the report is

    A. III, V, IV, II, I   B. III, II, V, IV, I
    C. III, IV, I, II, V   D. III, II, IV, I, V

10. Police Officer Franco is completing a report of an assault. The report will contain the following five sentences: 10._____

    I. In the park I observed an elderly man lying on the ground, bleeding from a back wound.

    II. I applied first aid to control the bleeding and radioed for an ambulance to respond.

    III. The elderly man stated that he was sitting on the park bench when he was attacked from behind by two males.

    IV. I received a report of a man's screams coming from inside the park, and I went to investigate.

    V. The old man could not give a description of his attackers.

The MOST logical order for the above sentences to appear in the report is

A. IV, I, II, III, V   B. V, III, I, IV, II
C. IV, III, V, II, I   D. II, I, V, IV, III

11. Police Officer Williams is completing a Crime Report. The report contains the following five sentences:

    I. As Police Officer Hanson and I approached the store, we noticed that the front door was broken.

    II. After determining that the burglars had fled, we notified the precinct of the burglary.

    III. I walked through the front door as Police Officer Hanson walked around to the back.

    IV. At approximately midnight, an alarm was heard at the Apex Jewelry Store.

    V. We searched the store and found no one.

The MOST logical order for the above sentences to appear in the report is

A. I, IV, II, III, V   B. I, IV, III, V, II
C. IV, I, III, II, V   D. IV, I, III, V, II

12. Police Officer Clay is giving a report to the news media regarding someone who has jumped from the Empire State Building. His report will include the following five sentences:

    I. I responded to the 86th floor, where I found the person at the edge of the roof.

    II. A security guard at the building had reported that a man was on the roof at the 86th floor.

    III. At 5:30 P.M., the person jumped from the building.

    IV. I received a call from the radio dispatcher at 4:50 P.M. to respond to the Empire State Building.

    V. I tried to talk to the person and convince him not to jump.

The MOST logical order for the above sentences to appear in the report is

A. I, II, IV, III, V   B. III, IV, I, II, V
C. II, IV, I, III, V   D. IV, II, I, V, III

13. The following five sentences are part of a report of a burglary written by Police Officer Reed:

    I. When I arrived at 2400 1st Avenue, I noticed that the door was slightly open.

    II. I yelled out, *Police, don't move!*

    III. As I entered the apartment, I saw a man with a TV set passing it through a window to another man standing on a fire escape.

    IV. While on foot patrol, I was informed by the radio dispatcher that a burglary was in progress at 2400 1st Avenue.

    V. However, the burglars quickly ran down the fire escape.

The MOST logical order for the above sentences to appear in the report is

A. I, III, IV, V, II   B. IV, I, III, V, II
C. IV, I, III, II, V   D. I, IV, III, II, V

14. Police Officer Jenkins is preparing a report for Lost or Stolen Property. The report will   14.____
include the following five sentences:
    I.   On the stairs, Mr. Harris slipped on a wet leaf and fell on the landing.
    II. It wasn't until he got to the token booth that Mr. Harris realized his wallet was no longer in his back pants pocket.
    III. A boy wearing a football jersey helped him up and brushed off the back of Mr. Harris' pants.
    IV. Mr. Harris states he was walking up the stairs to the elevated subway at Queensborough Plaza.
    V. Before Mr. Harris could thank him, the boy was running down the stairs to the street.

The MOST logical order for the above sentences to appear in the report is

   A. IV, III, V, I, II   B. IV, I, III, V, II
   C. I, IV, II, III, V   D. I, II, IV, III, V

15. Police Officer Hubbard is completing a report of a missing person. The report will contain   15.____
the following five sentences:
    I.   I visited the store at 7:55 P.M. and asked the employees if they had seen a girl fitting the description I had been given.
    II. She gave me a description and said she had gone into the local grocery store at about 6:15 P.M.
    III. I asked the woman for a description of her daughter.
    IV. The distraught woman called the precinct to report that her daughter, aged 12, had not returned from an errand.
    V. The storekeeper said a girl matching the description had been in the store earlier, but he could not give an exact time.

The MOST logical order for the above sentences to appear in the report is

   A. I, III, II, V, IV   B. IV, III, II, I, V
   C. V, I, II, III, IV   D. III, I, II, IV, V

16. A police officer is completing an entry in his Daily Activity Log regarding traffic sum-   16.____
monses which he issued. The following five sentences will be included in the entry:
    I.   I was on routine patrol parked 16 yards west of 170th Street and Clay Avenue.
    II. The summonses were issued for unlicensed operator and disobeying a steady red light.
    III. At 8 A.M. hours, I observed an auto traveling westbound on 170th Street not stop for a steady red light at the intersection of Clay Avenue and 170th Street.
    IV. I stopped the driver of the auto and determined that he did not have a valid driver's license.
    V. After a brief conversation, I informed the motorist that he was receiving two summonses.

The MOST logical order for the above sentences to appear in the report is

   A. I, III, IV, V, II   B. III, IV, II, V, I
   C. V, II, I, III, IV   D. IV, V, II, I, III

17. The following sentences appeared on an Incident Report: 17.___
    I. Three teenagers who had been ejected from the theater were yelling at patrons who were now entering.
    II. Police Officer Dixon told the teenagers to leave the area.
    III. The teenagers said that they were told by the manager to leave the theater because they were talking during the movie.
    IV. The theater manager called the precinct at 10:20 P.M. to report a disturbance outside the theater.
    V. A patrol car responded to the theater at 10:42 P.M. and two police officers went over to the teenagers.

The MOST logical order for the above sentences to appear in the Incident Report

A. I, V, IV, III, II   B. IV, I, V, III, II
C. IV, I, III, V, II   D. IV, III, I, V, II

18. Activity Log entries are completed by police officers. Police Officer Samuels has written   18.___
an entry concerning vandalism and part of it contains the following five sentences:
    I. The man, in his early twenties, ran down the block and around the corner.
    II. A man passing the store threw a brick through a window of the store.
    III. I arrived on the scene and began to question the witnesses about the incident.
    IV. Malcolm Holmes, the owner of the Fast Service Shoe Repair Store, was working in the back of the store at approximately 3 P.M.
    V. After the man fled, Mr. Holmes called the police.

The MOST logical order for the above sentences to appear in the Activity Log is

A. IV, II, I, V, III   B. II, IV, I, III, V
C. II, I, IV, III, V   D. IV, II, V, III, I

19. Police Officer Buckley is preparing a report concerning a dispute in a restaurant. The   19.___
report will contain the following five sentences:
    I. The manager, Charles Chin, and a customer, Edward Green, were standing near the register arguing over the bill.
    II. The manager refused to press any charges providing Green pay the check and leave.
    III. While on foot patrol, I was informed by a passerby of a disturbance in the Dragon Flame Restaurant.
    IV. Green paid the $7.50 check and left the restaurant.
    V. According to witnesses, the customer punched the owner in the face when Chin asked him for the amount due.

The MOST logical order for the above sentences to appear in the report is

A. III, I, V, II, IV   B. I, II, III, IV, V
C. V, I, III, II, IV   D. III, V, II, IV, I

20. Police Officer Wilkins is preparing a report for leaving the scene of an accident. The report will include the following five sentences:

    I. The Dodge struck the right rear fender of Mrs. Smith's 1980 Ford and continued on its way.
    II. Mrs. Smith stated she was making a left turn from 40th Street onto Third Avenue.
    III. As the car passed, Mrs. Smith noticed the dangling rear license plate #412AEJ.
    IV. Mrs. Smith complained to police of back pains and was removed by ambulance to Bellevue Hospital.
    V. An old green Dodge traveling up Third Avenue went through the red light at 40th Street and Third Avenue.

    The MOST logical order for the above sentences to appear in the report is

    A. V, III, I, II, IV
    C. IV, V, I, II, III
    B. I, III, II, V, IV
    D. II, V, I, III, IV

    20._____

21. Detective Simon is completing a Crime Report. The report contains the following five sentences:

    I. Police Officer Chin, while on foot patrol, heard the yelling and ran in the direction of the man.
    II. The man, carrying a large hunting knife, left the High Sierra Sporting Goods Store at approximately 10:30 A.M.
    III. When the man heard Police Officer Chin, he stopped, dropped the knife, and began to cry.
    IV. As Police Officer Chin approached the man, he drew his gun and yelled, *Police, freeze.*
    V. After the man left the store, he began yelling, over and over, *I am going to 'kill myself!*

    The MOST logical order for the above sentences to appear in the report is

    A. V, II, I, IV, III
    C. II, V, IV, I, III
    B. II, V, I, IV, III
    D. II, I, V, IV, III

    21._____

22. Police Officer Miller is preparing a Complaint Report which will include the following five sentences:

    I. From across the lot, he yelled to the boys to get away from his car.
    II. When he came out of the store, he noticed two teenage boys trying to break into his car.
    III. The boys fled as Mr. Johnson ran to his car.
    IV. Mr. Johnson stated that he parked his car in the municipal lot behind Tams Department Store.
    V. Mr. Johnson saw that the door lock had been broken, but nothing was missing from inside the auto.

    The MOST logical order for the above sentences to appear in the report is

    A. IV, I, II, V, III
    C. IV, II, I, III, V
    B. II, III, I, V, IV
    D. I, II, III, V, IV

    22._____

23. Police Officer O'Hara completes a Universal Summons for a motorist who has just   23.___
passed a red traffic light. The Universal Summons includes the following five sentences:
    I.   As the car passed the light, I followed in the patrol car.
    II.   After the driver stopped the car, he stated that the light was yellow, not red.
    III. A blue Cadillac sedan passed the red light on the corner of 79th Street and
        3rd Avenue at 11:25 P.M.
    IV. As a result, the driver was informed that he did pass a red light and that his
        brake lights were not working.
    V.   The driver in the Cadillac stopped his car as soon as he saw the patrol car,
        and I noticed that the brake lights were not working.
The MOST logical order for the above sentences to appear in the Universal Summons
is

    A.   I, III, V, II, IV   B.   III, I, V, II, IV
    C.   IiI, I, V, IV, II   D.   I, III, IV, II, V

24. Detective Egan is preparing a follow-up report regarding a homicide on 170th Street and   24.___
College Avenue. An unknown male was found at the scene. The report will contain the
following five sentences:
    I.   Police Officer Gregory wrote down the names, addresses, and phone num-
        bers of the witnesses.
    II.   A 911 operator received a call of a man shot and dispatched Police Officers
        Worth and Gregory to the scene.
    III. They discovered an unidentified male dead on the street.
    IV. Police Officer Worth notified the Precinct Detective Unit immediately.
    V.   At approximately 9:00 A.M., an unidentified male shot another male in the
        chest during an argument.
The MOST logical order for the above sentences to appear in the report is

    A.   V, II, III, IV, I   B.   II, III, V, IV, I
    C.   IV, I, V, II, III   D.   V, III, II, IV, I

25. Police Officer Tracey is preparing a Robbery Report which will include the following five   25.___
sentences:
    I.   I ran around the corner and observed a man pointing a gun at a taxidriver.
    II.   I informed the man I was a police officer and that he should not move.
    III. I was on the corner of 125th Street and Park Avenue when I heard a scream
        coming from around the corner.
    IV. The man turned around and fired one shot at me.
    V.   I fired once, shooting him in the arm and causing him to fall to the ground.
The MOST logical order for the above sentences to appear in the report is

    A.   I, III, IV, II, V   B.   IV, V, II, I, III
    C.   III, I, II, IV, V   D.   III, I, V, II, IV

KEY (CORRECT ANSWERS)

1. B	11. D
2. B	12. D
3. B	13. C
4. A	14. B
5. A	15. B
6. B	16. A
7. A	17. B
8. D	18. A
9. B	19. A
10. A	20. D

21. B
22. C
23. B
24. A
25. C

———

TEST 2

DIRECTIONS: The sentences that follow are in scrambled order. You are to rearrange them in proper order and indicate the letter choice containing the CORRECT answer. *PRINT THE LETTER OF THE CORRECT ANSWER IN THE SPACE AT THE RIGHT.*

1. Police Officer Weiker is completing a Complaint Report which will contain the following five sentences:

    I.   Mr. Texlor was informed that the owner of the van would receive a parking ticket and that the van would be towed away.

    II.   The police tow truck arrived approximately one half hour after Mr. Texlor complained.

    III.   While on foot patrol on West End Avenue, I saw the owner of Rand's Restaurant arrive to open his business.

    IV.   Mr. Texlor, the owner, called to me and complained that he could not receive deliveries because a van was blocking his driveway.

    V.   The van's owner later reported to the precinct that his van had been stolen, and he was then informed that it had been towed.

The MOST logical order for the above sentences to appear in the report is

    A.   III, V, I, II, IV   B.   III, IV, I, II, V
    C.   IV, III, I, II, V   D.   IV, III, II, I, V

2. Police Officer Ames is completing an entry in his Activity Log. The entry contains the following five sentences:

    I.   Mr. Sands gave me a complete description of the robber.

    II.   Alvin Sands, owner of the Star Delicatessen, called the precinct to report he had just been robbed.

    III.   I then notified all police patrol vehicles to look for a white male in his early twenties wearing brown pants and shirt, a black leather jacket, and black and white sneakers.

    IV.   I arrived on the scene after being notified by the precinct that a robbery had just occurred at the Star Delicatessen.

    V.   Twenty minutes later, a man fitting the description was arrested by a police officer on patrol six blocks from the delicatessen.

The MOST logical order for the above sentences to appear in the Activity Log is

    A.   II, I, IV, III, V   B.   II, IV, III, I, V
    C.   II, IV, I, III, V   D.   II, IV, I, V, III

3. Police Officer Benson is completing a Complaint Report concerning a stolen taxicab, which will include the following five sentences:

    I.   Police Officer Benson noticed that a cab was parked next to a fire hydrant.

    II.   Dawson *borrowed* the cab for transportation purposes since he was in a hurry.

    III.   Ed Dawson got into his car and tried to start it, but the battery was dead.

    IV.   When he reached his destination, he parked the cab by a fire hydrant and placed the keys under the seat.

    V.   He looked around and saw an empty cab with the engine running.

The MOST logical order for the above sentences to appear in the report is

A. I, III, II, IV, V   B. III, I, II, V, IV
C. III, V, II, IV, I   D. V, II, IV, III, I

4. Police Officer Hatfield is reviewing his Activity Log entry prior to completing a report. The   4.____
    entry contains the following five sentences:

    I. When I arrived at Zand's Jewelry Store, I noticed that the door was slightly open.
    II. I told the burglar I was a police officer and that he should stand still or he would be shot.
    III. As I entered the store, I saw a man wearing a ski mask attempting to open the safe in the back of the store.
    IV. On December 16, 1990, at 1:38 A.M., I was informed that a burglary was in progress at Zand's Jewelry Store on East 59th Street.
    V. The burglar quickly pulled a knife from his pocket when he saw me.

    The MOST logical order for the above sentences to appear in the report is

    A. IV, I, III, V, II   B. I, IV, III, V, II
    C. IV, III, II, V, I   D. I, III, IV, V, II

5. Police Officer Lorenz is completing a report of a murder. The report will contain the fol-   5.____
    lowing five statements made by a witness:

    I. I was awakened by the sound of a gunshot coming from the apartment next door, and I decided to check.
    II. I entered the apartment and looked into the kitchen and the bathroom.
    III. I found Mr. Hubbard's body slumped in the bathtub.
    IV. The door to the apartment was open, but I didn't see anyone.
    V. He had been shot in the head.

    The MOST logical order for the above sentences to appear in the report is

    A. I, III, II, IV, V   B. I, IV, II, III, V
    C. IV, II, I, III, V   D. III, I, II, IV, V

6. Police Officer Baldwin is preparing an accident report which will include the following five   6.____
    sentences:

    I. The old man lay on the ground for a few minutes, but was not physically hurt.
    II. Charlie Watson, a construction worker, was repairing some brick work at the top of a building at 54th Street and Madison Avenue.
    III. Steven Green, his partner, warned him that this could be dangerous, but Watson ignored him.
    IV. A few minutes later, one of the bricks thrown by Watson smashed to the ground in front of an old man, who fainted out of fright.
    V. Mr. Watson began throwing some of the bricks over the side of the building.

    The MOST logical order for the above sentences to appear in the report is

    A. II, V, III, IV, I   B. I, IV, II, V, III
    C. III, II, IV, V, I   D. II, III, I, IV, V

7. Police Officer Porter is completing an incident report concerning her rescue of a woman being held hostage by a former boyfriend. Her report will contain the following five sentences:

    I.   I saw a man holding .25 caliber gun to a woman's head, but he did not see me.

    II.   I then broke a window and gained access to the house.

    III.   As I approached the house on foot, a gunshot rang out and I heard a woman scream.

    IV.   A decoy van brought me as close as possible to the house where the woman was being held hostage.

    V.   I ordered the man to drop his gun, and he released the woman and was taken into custody.

The MOST logical order for the above sentences to appear in the report is

    A.   I, III, II, IV, V   B.   IV, III, II, I, V
    C.   III, II, I, IV, V   D.   V, I, II, III, IV

8. Police Officer Byrnes is preparing a crime report concerning a robbery. The report will consist of the following five sentences:

    I.   Mr. White, following the man's instructions, opened the car's hood, at which time the man got out of the auto, drew a revolver, and ordered White to give him all the money in his pockets.

    II.   Investigation has determined there were no witnesses to this incident.

    III.   The man asked White to check the oil and fill the tank.

    IV.   Mr. White, a gas attendant, states that he was working alone at the gas station when a black male pulled up to the gas pump in a white Mercury.

    V.   White was then bound and gagged by the male and locked in the gas station's rest room.

The MOST logical order for the above sentences to appear in the report is

    A.   IV, I, III, II, V   B.   III, I, II, V, IV
    C.   IV, III, I, V, II   D.   I, III, IV, II, V

9. Police Officer Gale is preparing a report of a crime committed against Mr. Weston. The report will consist of the following five sentences:

    I.   The man, who had a gun, told Mr. Weston not to scream for help and ordered him back into the apartment.

    II.   With Mr. Weston disposed of in this fashion, the man proceeded to ransack the apartment.

    III.   Opening the door to see who was there, Mr. Weston was confronted by a tall white male wearing a dark blue jacket and white pants.

    IV.   Mr. Weston was at home alone in his living room when the doorbell rang.

    V.   Once inside, the man bound and gagged Mr. Weston and locked him in the bathroom.

The MOST logical order for the above sentences to appear in the report is

    A.   III, V, II, I, IV   B.   IV, III, I, V, II
    C.   III, V, IV, II, I   D.   IV, III, V, I, II

10. A police officer is completing a report of a robbery, which will contain the following five sentences: 10.____
    I. Two police officers were about to enter the Red Rose Coffee Shop on 47th Street and 8th Avenue.
    II. They then noticed a male running up the street carrying a brown paper bag.
    III. They heard a woman standing outside the Broadway Boutique yelling that her store had just been robbed by a young man, and she was pointing up the street.
    IV. They caught up with him and made an arrest.
    V. The police officers pursued the male, who ran past them on 8th Avenue.

    The MOST logical order for the above sentences to appear in the report is

    A. I, III, II, V, IV   B. III, I, II, V, IV
    C. IV, V, I, II, III   D. I, V, IV, III, II

11. Police Officer Capalbo is preparing a report of a bank robbery. The report will contain the following five statements made by a witness: 11.____
    I. Initially, all I could see were two men, dressed in maintenance uniforms, sitting in the area reserved for bank officers.
    II. I was passing the bank at 8 P.M. and noticed that all the lights were out, except in the rear section.
    III. Then I noticed two other men in the bank, coming from the direction of the vault, carrying a large metal box.
    IV. At this point, I decided to call the police.
    V. I knocked on the window to get the attention of the men in the maintenance uniforms, and they chased the two men carrying the box down a flight of steps.

    The MOST logical order for the above sentences to appear in the report is

    A. IV, I, II, V, III   B. I, III, II, V, IV
    C. II, I, III, V, IV   D. II, III, I, V, IV

12. Police Officer Roberts is preparing a crime report concerning an assault and a stolen car. The report will contain the following five sentences: 12.____
    I. Upon leaving the store to return to his car, Winters noticed that a male unknown to him was sitting in his car.
    II. The man then re-entered Winters' car and drove away, fleeing north on 2nd Avenue.
    III. Mr. Winters stated that he parked his car in front of 235 East 25th Street and left the engine running while he went into the butcher shop at that location.
    IV. Mr. Robert Gering, a witness, stated that the male is known in the neighborhood as Bobby Rae and is believed to reside at 323 East 114th Street.
    V. When Winters approached the car and ordered the man to get out, the man got out of the auto and struck Winters with his fists, knocking him to the ground.

    The MOST logical order for the above sentences to appear in the report is

    A. III, II, V, I, IV   B. III, I, V, II, IV
    C. I, IV, V, II, III   D. III, II, I, V, IV

13. Police Officer Robinson is preparing a crime report concerning the robbery of Mr. Edwards' store. The report will consist of the following five sentences:

    I.   When the last customer left the store, the two men drew revolvers and ordered Mr. Edwards to give them all the money in the cash register.

    II.   The men proceeded to the back of the store as if they were going to do some shopping.

    III. Janet Morley, a neighborhood resident, later reported that she saw the men enter a green Ford station wagon and flee northbound on Albany Avenue.

    IV. Edwards complied after which the gunmen ran from the store.

    V.   Mr. Edwards states that he was stocking merchandise behind the store counter when two white males entered the store.

The MOST logical order for the above sentences to appear in the report is

    A. V, II, III, I, IV   B. V, II, I, IV, III
    C. II, I, V, IV, III   D. III, V, II, I, IV

14. Police Officer Wendell is preparing an accident report for a 6-car accident that occurred at the intersection of Bath Avenue and Bay Parkway. The report will consist of the following five sentences:

    I.   A 2006 Volkswagen Beetle, traveling east on Bath Avenue, swerved to the left to avoid the Impala, and struck a 2004 Ford station wagon which was traveling west on Bath Avenue.

    II.   The Seville then mounted the curb on the northeast corner of Bath Avenue and Bay Parkway and struck a light pole.

    III. A 2003 Buick Lesabre, traveling northbound on Bay Parkway directly behind the Impala, struck the Impala, pushing it into the intersection of Bath Avenue and Bay Parkway.

    IV. A 2005 Chevy Impala, traveling northbound on Bay Parkway, had stopped for a red light at Bath Avenue.

    V.   A 2007 Toyota, traveling westbound on Bath Avenue, swerved to the right to avoid hitting the Ford station wagon, and struck a 2007 Cadillac Seville double-parked near the corner.

The MOST logical order for the above sentences to appear in the report is

    A. IV, III, V, II, I   B. III, IV, V, II, I
    C. IV, III, I, V, II   D. III, IV, V, I, II

15. The following five sentences are part of an Activity Log entry Police Officer Rogers made regarding an explosion,

    I.   I quickly treated the pedestrian for the injury.

    II.   The explosion caused a glass window in an office building to shatter.

    III. After the pedestrian was treated, a call was placed to the precinct requesting additional police officers to evacuate the area.

    IV. After all the glass settled to the ground, I saw a pedestrian who was bleeding from the arm

    V.   While on foot patrol near 5th Avenue and 53rd Street, I heard a loud explosion.

The MOST logical order for the above sentences to appear in the report is

    A. II, V, IV, I, III   B. V, II, IV, III, I
    C. V, II, I, IV, III   D. V, II, IV, I, III

16. Police Officer David is completing a report regarding illegal activity near the entrance to   16.____
Madison Square Garden during a recent rock concert. The report will contain the following five sentences:
    I. As I came closer to the man, he placed what appeared to be tickets in his
pocket and began to walk away.
    II. After the man stopped, I questioned him about *scalping* tickets.
    III. While on assignment near the Madison Square Garden entrance, I observed
a man apparently selling tickets.
    IV. I stopped the man by stating that I was a police officer.
    V. The man was then given a summons, and he left the area.
The MOST logical order for the above sentences to appear in the report is

    A. I, III, IV, II, V   B. III, I, IV, V, II
    C. III, IV, I, II, V   D. III, I, IV, II, V

17. Police Officer Sampson is preparing a report concerning a dispute in a bar. The report   17.____
will contain the following five sentences:
    I. John Evans, the bartender, ordered the two men out of the bar.
    II. Two men dressed in dungarees entered the C and D Bar at 5:30 P.M.
    III. The two men refused to leave and began to beat up Evans.
    IV. A customer in the bar saw me on patrol and yelled to me to come separate
the three men.
    V. The two men became very drunk and loud within a short time.
The MOST logical order for the above sentences to appear in the report is

    A. II, I, V, III, IV   B. II, III, IV, V, I
    C. III, I, II, V, IV   D. II, V, I, III, IV

18. A police officer is completing a report concerning the response to a crime in progress.   18.____
The report will include the following five sentences:
    I. The officers saw two armed men run out of the liquor store and into a waiting
car.
    II. Police Officers Lunty and Duren received the call and responded to the liquor
store.
    III. The robbers gave up without a struggle.
    IV. Lunty and Duren blocked the getaway car with their patrol car.
    V. A call came into the precinct concerning a robbery in progress at Jane's
Liquor Store.
The MOST logical order for the above sentences to appear in the report is

    A. V, II, I, IV, III   B. II, V, I, III, IV
    C. V, I, IV, II, III   D. I, V, II, III, IV

19. Police Officer Jenkins is preparing a Crime Report which will consist of the following five   19.____
sentences:
    I. After making inquiries in the vicinity, Smith found out that his next door neigh-
bor, Viola Jones, had seen two local teenagers, Michael Heinz and Vincent
Gaynor, smash his car's windshields with a crowbar.
    II. Jones told Smith that the teenagers live at 8700 19th Avenue.
    III. Mr. Smith heard a loud crash at approximately 11:00 P.M., looked out his
apartment window, and saw two white males running away from his car.
    IV. Smith then reported the incident to the precinct, and Heinz and Gaynor were
arrested at the address given.

V. Leaving his apartment to investigate further, Smith discovered that his car's front and rear windshields had been smashed.

The MOST logical order for the above sentences to appear in the report is

A. III, IV, V, I, II
C. III, I, V, II, IV

B. III, V, I, II, IV
D. V, III, I, II, IV

20. Sergeant Nancy Winston is reviewing a Gun Control Report which will contain the following five sentences:

I. The man fell to the floor when hit in the chest with three bullets from 22 caliber gun.
II. Merriam'22 caliber gun was seized, and he wasgiven a summons for not having a pistol permit.
III. Christopher Merriam, the owner of A-Z Grocery, shot a man who attempted to rob him.
IV. Police Officer Franks responded and asked Merriam for his pistol permit, which he could not produce.
V. Merriam phoned the police to report he had just shot a man who had attempted to rob him.

The MOST logical order for the above sentences to appear in the report is

A. III, I, V, IV, II
C. III, I, V, II, IV

B. I, III, V, IV, II
D. I, III, II, V, IV

21. Detective John Manville is completing a report for his superior regarding the murder of an unknown male who was shot in Central Park. The report will contain the following five sentences:

I. Police Officers Langston and Cavers responded to the scene.
II. I received the assignment to investigate the murder in Central Park from Detective Sergeant Rogers.
III. Langston notified the Detective Bureau after questioning Jason.
IV. An unknown male, apparently murdered, was discovered in Central Park by Howard Jason, a park employee, who immediately called the police.
V. Langston and Cavers questioned Jason.

The MOST logical order for the above sentences to appear in the report is

A. I, IV, V, III, II
C. IV, I, V, III, II

B. IV, I, V, II, III
D. IV, V, I, III, II

22. A police officer is completing a report concerning the arrest of a juvenile. The report will contain the following five sentences:

I. Sanders then telephoned Jay's parents from the precinct to inform them of their son's arrest.
II. The store owner resisted, and Jay then shot him and ran from the store.
III. Jay was transported directly to the precinct by Officer Sanders.
IV. James Jay, a juvenile, walked into a candy store and announced a hold-up.
V. Police Officer Sanders, while on patrol, arrested Jay a block from the candy store.

The MOST logical order for the above sentences to appear in the report is

A. IV, V, II, I, III
C. II, IV, V, III, I

B. IV, II, V, III, I
D. V, IV, II, I, III

23. Police Officer Olsen prepared a crime report for a robbery which contained the following   23._____
five sentences:

    I.   Mr. Gordon was approached by this individual who then produced a gun and demanded the money from the cash register.

    II.   The man then fled from the scene on foot, southbound on 5th Avenue.

    III.   Mr. Gordon was working at the deli counter when a white male, 5'6", 150-160 lbs., wearing a green jacket and blue pants, entered the store.

    IV.   Mr. Gordon complied with the man's demands and handed him the daily receipts.

    V.   Further investigation has determined there are no other witnesses to this robbery.

The MOST logical order for the above sentences to appear in the report is

    A.   I, III, IV, V, II   B.   I, IV, II, III, V
    C.   III, IV, I, V, II   D.   III, I, IV, , II, V

24. Police Officer Bryant responded to 285 E. 31st Street to take a crime report of a burglary   24._____
of Mr. Bond's home. The report will contain a brief description of the incident, consisting
of the following five sentences:

    I.   When Mr. Bond attempted to stop the burglar by grabbing him, he was pushed to the floor.

    II.   The burglar had apparently gained access to the home by forcing open the 2nd floor bedroom window facing the fire escape.

    III.   Mr. Bond sustained a head injury in the scuffle, and the burglar exited the home through the front door.

    IV.   Finding nothing in the dresser, the burglar proceeded downstairs to the first floor, where he was confronted by Mr. Bond who was reading in the dining room.

    V.   Once inside, he searched the drawers of the bedroom dresser.

The MOST logical order for the above sentences to appear in the report is

    A.   V, IV, I, II, III   B.   II, V, IV, I, III
    C.   II, IV, V, III, I   D.   III, II, I, V, IV

25. Police Officer Derringer responded to a call of a rape-homicide case in his patrol area   25._____
and was ordered to prepare an incident report, which will contain the following five sentences:

    I.   He pushed Miss Scott to the ground and forcibly raped her.

    II.   Mary Scott was approached from behind by a white male, 5'7", 150-160 lbs. wearing dark pants and a white jacket.

    III.   As Robinson approached the male, he ordered him to stop.

    IV.   Screaming for help, Miss Scott alerted one John Robinson, a local grocer, who chased her assailant as he fled the scene.

    V.   The male turned and fired two shots at Robinson, who fell to the ground mortally wounded.

The MOST logical order for the above' sentences to appear in the report is

    A.   IV, III, I, II, V   B.   II, IV, III, V, I
    C.   II, IV, I, V, III   D.   II, I, IV, III, V

KEY (CORRECT ANSWERS)

1.	B	11.	C
2.	C	12.	B
3.	C	13.	B
4.	A	14.	C
5.	B	15.	D
6.	A	16.	D
7.	B	17.	D
8.	C	18.	A
9.	B	19.	B
10.	A	20.	A

21.	C
22.	B
23.	D
24.	B
25.	D